My Excuses Are Killing Me

How to be productive and
successful without sacrificing
who you are

Nijel James

Copyright

© Copyright 2022 Nijel James. All Rights Reserved. Copyright protected with ProtectMyWork.com Reference Number: 17226170422S021.

No permission is given for any part of this book to be reproduced, transmitted in any form, or means, electronic or mechanical, stored in a retrieval system, photocopied, recorded, scanned, or otherwise. Any of these actions require the proper written permission of the publisher.

A word from the author

You're writing that report containing a few proposals that might or might not become policies. You're trying to make it look pithy, compelling, critical, and convincing all at the same time. You want your boss to approve of your work. You're busy. That's a fact. But are you productive? Maybe. Does being busy equal being productive? It depends. To a busy person, a successful day is determined by the number of hours worked. To a productive person, success is indicated by the number of tasks crossed off the to-do list.

To be successful - financially, socially, personally - we must do things. It's not just about doing anything. Success is about doing the RIGHT things. Think about it.

What's your definition of success? Having a job? Doing well in school? Winning awards in sports? Being a celebrity or a politician or a media personality or an actor in a TV show? Whichever definition of success you believe in, you must do the RIGHT things to achieve it.

An epiphany came to me as I was huffing and puffing in the middle of my bed. I was simply lying flat on my back, doing nothing. Lying down flat, I realized, is one of the easiest and most productive things that you can actually do. Some people call it sleeping. Others call it resting or meditating or just plain old relaxation. But it is indeed one of life's easiest - perhaps THE easiest - form of productivity! Amusing, isn't it? We can be most productive when we're doing nothing but taking a short break from our busy lives to reflect.

In that moment of reflection, I realized something: Productivity isn't measured by the number of hours we spend on a task. To a car salesman, the only thing that truly matters is the number of deals closed in that month; not the number of clients that didn't buy or how close he was to sealing the deal. To a teacher, it's a matter of the number of students who passed the exam and not how many students failed to show up or how he was able to make all his lessons so interesting that the kids actually WANTED to come back for more.

To a business executive, it's all about the number of deals closed, not the number of hours worked. To a politician, it's all about how many votes he got and not what might have been said if he had only given the speech after all. At that moment, I realized that productivity is measured by an entirely different metric: the number of things done. I'm writing this book for three things. First, it's the manual I wish I had when I was on the brink of accepting a life of busyness. Working two jobs and going to school full-time and pursuing my goals in between would have been a lot more bearable if I were better equipped with the right tools. In that regard, this book is what I'd want to read.

Maybe you need a gentle nudge to make a change. Perhaps you're not sure if you really want to make any changes. Perhaps you need more convincing. But do read on and see where I'm coming from.

Second, this book is written for those who want to get back what's lost in their busy lives. What would it be like if your schedule were decluttered? How much of your potential would you recover? Would you be wiser, richer, happier?

I hope this book will inspire you to change for the better. If my reasoning doesn't convince you, maybe it'll push - or even shove - you into making a change, or at least consider doing so.

Finally, I want you to see the other side of the coin. I'd like to show you that it's not productive to be busy all the time. It's not advisable. You don't have to work yourself so hard that you neglect things that are most important in life, like relationships with family and friends, your health, and just plain old relaxation.

The tips, techniques and systems in this book have worked for me, for my friends, for my family and even for my clients. They will work for you too. I guarantee you that if you take action, you'll see results. This book is based on one simple principle: To get more things done by figuring out what your future self will thank you for. The knowledge contained in this book will remain to be a form of entertainment until you choose to take action. It's not that self-help books don't work. They do. But what we want is effortless self-improvement. If I had a magic wand that would turn anyone into a workhorse that never sleeps, never gets tired and crushes the competition, I would be rich. I ask that you follow the ideas in this book, even just for a month, and see whatever magic happens.

There is a lot to learn here, all of which you can easily put into practice starting today. Congratulations. By picking up this book, you've demonstrated that you are ready to get more things done. Let's do this. You'll rock.

Cheers,

Nijel James

About the Author

Nijel James is a prolific writer and filmmaker, specializing in business, self-help, and productivity. A recipient of numerous awards, Nijel has worked across multiple continents running his own businesses. As an entrepreneur he has also trained large numbers of people on productivity and business success. He enjoys the challenge of teaching others to be more productive, with the ultimate goal being an increased quality of life for the reader. He is driven by this passion and loves to share what he learns.

In the last 20 years he has come to learn that a healthy balance between work and life is key to a healthy, happy, and prosperous life.

Nijel's book My Excuses are Killing Me, is an effort at writing for the general public and it is a collection of his wisdom, knowledge and experience. It is packed with priceless tips for any small business, entrepreneur or anyone looking to make their life easier. It is a book that he wishes someone had given him when he was starting out on his career path, as he believes it will help him remain balanced with work and life for many years to come.

How to use this book

For your future self

Time is linear. Yesterday is gone. Tomorrow is not yet here. Today is the only time you really have. I'm not asking you to use it wisely. No. I want to give you a different view of it. In three years from now, you will look back. There are things that you'll wish you did, things you wish you said and things you wish had happened differently. You're probably doing all three right now. I know I am. The thing about time is that it only flows one way. It can't be recaptured. There's no dial to turn back to go over past events and make certain that certain things were done a little better, or a little more aggressively, or with a little more oomph.

You're not doing it for yourself. You're doing it for your future self. Your future self will be grateful that you didn't come home from that business trip only to find a week of unwashed clothes. Future you will be glad that you had the discipline to make it to that one last meeting before heading home. Future you will be grateful for the things you said, but never did. Future you will thank your past self for making the hard decisions today, so that tomorrow will be a whole lot easier.

This book is about helping your future self be able to look back on today and say, "*thank you.*" Think about it like this: Your life is one big story - sort of like a novel or a movie. The constant struggle is to keep readers (yourself) engaged. We're distracted, we're tempted to jump ahead, and sometimes we just forget to finish the story. Your future self knows that you can't change the past. All you can do is write down the next paragraph of this story. That's why right now, I want you to adopt a different mindset. You're not doing it for yourself. You're doing it for your future self. Tomorrow's You is a compilation of time management techniques, productivity hacks and motivation to achieve your goals. This book will work for you if:

- You have a lot on your plate and want to get more things done.

- You don't know where to start or what to do.

- You want practical advice on how to live a minimalist lifestyle.

- You want the power of positive habits that can change your life in the next 90 days... without pain or suffering.

- If you secretly feel like you're wasting time at work, even though you're working hard, every day.

This book is not for you if:

- You refuse to learn from others' experiences.

- You think knowledge is a burden.

- You don't think you need a helping hand.

- You believe that knowing your goals will magically turn them into reality in the next 60 days.

If you're sold on these ideas and want to get started right away, then scroll down to the next section and I'll tell you what to do. If not, please stay with me a little longer because there is one more thing I need to discuss: The mindset that willpower you though this journey... without pain or suffering... without any effort on your behalf at all.

The risk-taker. The supervisor and the doer.

In the corporate world, we have technicians, managers, and entrepreneurs. The technicians are the handy guys who work on the production line. They know their role inside out and they are incredibly good at what they do. To them, productivity is determined by the number of hours they spend at their desks cold calling leads, in the field installing equipment, driving around in an SUV or a booth, soldering a circuit board. They do all the grunt work so that their boss could have more time to think about his future goals and make his most important decisions.

The managers are the ones who help the technicians get their job done by holding everyone accountable to the vision of the company and by making sure things go smoothly. They assign tasks and make decisions in a systematic manner, using the processes and systems that have been in place for years. And they're still amazingly productive because they know how to delegate tasks, they know the right questions to ask and they're always thinking one step ahead.

The entrepreneurs are different. They're the guys who wake up every morning with a new idea of how to make the company more efficient or how to grow faster. Their ideas are innovative. They're always trying to find a new way to improve things. An entrepreneur is the guy who thinks outside of the box - always looking for ways to turn an obstacle into an opportunity and make things happen that others never thought were possible. To him, productivity is determined by his ability to disrupt industries and make people think differently.

Whatever position you're in right now, you must juggle between these three roles. In the second chapter of this book, "*The big picture*", you'll be the entrepreneur. You will learn how to delegate time spent on non-critical activities, how to define your goals and how to use them as a compass for your future decisions. Next, you will be the manager. You'll learn what systems are in place and why are they important; you will learn the basics of time management and accountability. And then, you'll be the technician. You will learn a few handy tips on how to be more productive while doing your current job. By following these 3 steps, I guarantee you that no matter what stage of life you're in right now (basically whatever role you're performing at work), tomorrow's You will have everything it needs to master productivity.

It's not just about being productive at the workplace, it's about becoming productive in every aspect of your life. It's not just about increasing your income, it's about finding peace, happiness, and fulfillment in life.

I have spent the last decade studying what makes people successful and happy. I have read almost a hundred books and articles on personal development, read the blogs of some of the most influential people in business, interviewed dozens of successful individuals from all walks of life (CEOs, entrepreneurs, fitness gurus), attended conferences and seminars - I've even tried some "get rich quick" schemes as well. And I'm now ready to share everything with you. Will you join me? Get ready to conquer your productivity.

What you'll learn in this book

We'll start by getting an updated picture of your life. I'll show you how to write down your goals, so that they can guide the decisions you make day in, day out. Then we'll figure out what's distracting you. You'll learn how to identify which activities are worth your time, and which are not. In order to do that, we'll be doing a review of Maslow's pyramid of needs after which I will give you a handy tool called the funnel of productivity that will help you figure out what activities bring the most value to your life and career and are worth spending time on.

You'll see how you can 'trick' your brain into believing that you're already at your peak performance, so you'll be able to make full use of your time and energy. You'll learn how to identify the four functions of our brain

- the neocortex: stimulus-centric, logical and analytical.

- the limbic system: emotional and instinctual.

- the reptilian brain: bodily needs and movements.

- and the fetal brain: self-oriented, vulnerable, and irrational. By using these 4 functions as a starting point for your decisions, you will no longer let people or things distract you from reaching the goals that matter most to you.

While you're preparing your mind for productivity, we'll take a look at your body as well. I'll show you how muscle memory has a huge impact on your productivity - why we instinctively garb our phones with our thumbs, why multitasking is a myth, why we're always late and why we don't have time for the things that matter most.

Then I'll break it down for you step by step. You'll learn how to use your time more effectively, so that you can have enough time to love your family and do the things you enjoy. By the end of this book, you'll have everything it takes to completely master your productivity. You'll know what gets your energy up, what keeps you going when things get tough and most importantly, why those things matter.

Contents

Copyright 2
A word from the author 3
About the Author 6
How to use this book 7
    For your future self 7
    The risk-taker. The supervisor and the doer 8
What you'll learn in this book 11
Introduction 18
    Momentum: A lesson from Isaac Newton 18
CHAPTER 1: THE BRIDGE 20
    A Reality check 20
    Taking stock of where you are in life 22
    Excuses: The lies we tell ourselves 23
    The fundamentals we'll be working on 26
    What if I'm still not happy? 28
    What can I do today to help myself be happier? 28
    The chains holding you back 29
CHAPTER 2: THE BIG PICTURE 31
    Where you want to be 31
    An exercise on visualization 33
    Success is subjective 35
    Your SMART goals 36
    Goal 1: I want to get my weight in control 37
    A positive environment 38
    Making the plan 40

13

CHAPTER 3: OUR TOOLKIT 42
   A pomodoro timer 42
   Sleep, food and hydration 44
   Positive self-talk 45
   A journal 46
   The night before routine 47
   Decisions on auto-pilot 48

CHAPTER 4: YOUR TIME 51
   Prioritizing tasks 52
   When to-do lists don't work 53
   Breaking down projects into tasks 54
   Breaking down projects into tasks 54
   Setting deadlines for yourself 56
   The ever-changing to-do list 57
   Dividing your day into work periods 58
   Taking a break 59

CHAPTER 5: HABITS 62
   How habits came to be 62
   Good habits and bad habits 63
   The three phases of a habit 64
   Good habit: Exercising every day 65
   Good habit: Drinking lots of water 66
   Good habit: Writing a gratitude list 67
   Good habit: Managing your time well 67
   Bad habit: Drinking alcohol after a long day 68
   Bad habit: Procrastinating 69

Bad habit: Fidgeting 69
Why is it hard to break a bad habit? 70
Breaking a bad habit 71
Habit Reversal Therapy 73
A Habit and a routine working together 74

CHAPTER 6: A ROUTINE THAT WORKS FOR YOU 76
What's a routine? 76
A daily routine that works for you 77
Your Productivity sweet spot 81
A winning morning routine 81
Your evening routine 82
The weekend routine 84

CHAPTER 7: PRODUCTIVITY 90
The productivity triangle: balancing Time, Energy and Focus
.... 91
Productivity at the workplace 93
Productivity when working from home 98
Applying The Pareto principle 103
The multitasking myth 105

CHAPTER 8: PROCRASTINATION 109
We don't procrastinate because we're lazy 109
Willpower or discipline? 112
The 10 minutes trick 113
Analysis paralysis 115
When it is okay to procrastinate 119

CHAPTER 9: BALANCING WORK AND LIFE 121
Why's balancing work and personal life important? 121

Working hard is not the same as working smart 123
A screen-free lunch break 124
Balancing work and family 126
Stress management 129
Learning to say no 130
Switching off from work 133

CHAPTER 10: DECLUTTERING 135
What's clutter? 137
What physical clutter does to our body 137
What physical clutter does to our mind 138
What it does to our money 138
The 4 types of Mental clutter 139
Negative self-talk 139
Getting rid of mental clutter 141
The minimalist game 143

CHAPTER 11: DITCH THE DISTRACTIONS 151
How do we overcome this?s 152
Identifying your distractions 154
Eliminating Digital distractions 155
How do we get rid of these distractions? 156
Improving your focus during meetings 158
Are emails distracting you? 160
Unprofessional, annoying and distracting co-workers 161

CHAPTER 12: RECHARGING 164
What's burnout? 164
Scheduling 'worry time' 166

Exercise for the body is music for the soul 167
  Recharging when you're emotionally drained 168
CHAPTER 13: STAYING ON TRACK 171
  Have an accountability system 171
  Handling failure and setbacks 173
  Getting back on track 177
Putting it all together 179
Appendix 182
  Phase 1: Ignorance 183
  Phase 2: Epiphany 183
  Phase 3: Action 184
  Phase 4: Mastery 184
Attribution 185

Introduction

Momentum: A lesson from Isaac Newton

Newton was a great, but very odd guy. The things he did were usually strange, and some of his beliefs seemed downright ridiculous to many people at the time. He invented calculus (yes, that crazy calculus), the binomial theorem and realized that Earth was not the center of the universe. He also discovered what we now call gravity. Funnily, the most important thing I learnt from his works isn't Physics 101. Instead, it's a lesson in productivity, momentum, and motivation that every human can learn from.

The first law of physics (the law of inertia) states that if an object is at rest, it will remain at rest unless acted on by an outside force. If you're in a state of inertia, something feels wrong; there's no motivation, no excitement and nothing driving you forward. Everything seems pointless and you're left with a constant feeling of lethargy. This is the opposite of momentum - when you have momentum, everything seems easy. The tasks that seemed so daunting yesterday are now a piece of cake today. You feel full of energy; motivation is high, and obstacles don't seem like obstacles anymore.

The law of inertia also teaches us that an object in motion tends to stay in motion unless acted on by an outside force. The moment we have momentum, the inertia is gone and there's no slowing down. We feel motivated, excited, and ready to take on the world - it doesn't matter if the world is coming at us or going away from us. We're always moving forward. This is what I like to call "*the activation energy.*" Once you've reached the activation energy, auto-pilot kicks in and you go through the motions without even thinking about it. Our reptilian brain is incredibly skilled at doing things that require little to no thinking. Once you've reached the activation energy, your reptilian brain takes over and keeps you going until the job is finished. We'll talk about this more later, but for now, know that the law of inertia (or lack thereof) is what makes momentum so very important.

CHAPTER 1: THE BRIDGE

It's time to reflect. Are you where you want to be? Be honest. Where are you on a scale of one to ten? A boring, old psychologist would ask if you're happy or sad. A banker would ask if your finances were in order. A gym trainer would ask if you were physically fit. A software developer would ask if you were productive. And so on... While all of these questions have their merits, I'd like to bring a slightly different perspective to this discussion.

In the beginning, we were perfect and free from the clutter of life's external goading. We were pure and untainted - like a snowflake or a newborn baby (okay, maybe not that much). As time goes by, we become more complex and "less pure," just as we become more crowded and complex as individuals. When we look back at our younger selves, it's not possible to find anything more pure than what we started out as.

<u>A reality check</u>

Before we start this self-help improvement journey, we must take stock of where we're at. How many hours do you spend at the workplace every day? Do you know how to get the most out of it? You might be doing a little bit of work at the office, but it doesn't necessarily mean you're getting better results. The best way to get a really good idea of your results is to take a realistic look at what you've been doing. The next step is to try and quantify those results.

So, coach yourself – how many hours do you spend in the workplace every day? How many are your productive hours / how much are you actually getting done? This can be measured by a few things:

a) How many hours are spent on 'wasted time'?

b) How many hours are spent on out of the office activities?

c) How much time is spent on communication and administration tasks? (Since these might not be directly related to work)

d) What portions of your day-to-day work are actually productive?

e) Are you really working on what you should be working on right now?

Take a realistic look at how much time you're spending in the office. Maybe you're at a 9 to 5 job but are you really working just 8 hours a day? You might be spending quite some time on non-work related matters.

Compare the total productive hours in a week. How much of it was spent on work? How much of it was spent on non-work related issues that could be cut away? Now look at the % of your days that you were actually productive. After you've assessed your situation, it's time to take control of your productivity.

Are you where you want to be? It's not just finances that help make a life happen, it's also about finding the right partner, ensuring that kids have time for each other, doing the things you love, having time to recharge after the day's fighting and the list goes on. There's a lot of conversation about the power of tracking your money, but it turns out that tracking your time is a lot more revealing about how you'll spend your life and whether that life will be anything like you'd hoped. Becoming aware of how we all allocate our time helps us make plans, get unstuck, and move forward.

Taking stock of where you are in life

Each one of us is a unique combination of goals, pressures, and circumstances. We each have to contort our lives in a different way to fit the puzzle pieces. Before we make plans, we should do some serious thinking about where we are, and how long we'll be there.

You can't change the past that's gone; but you can plan for the future. You should plan, in advance, for where you want your life to go. You need to identify what you want out of life. In order to make a good plan, you'll need to start by quantifying your current situation.

You'll need to take stock of the dreams you've let fall by the wayside, and of your current obligations (pets, family, jobs, etc.). Planning ahead is important because it gives you a chance to work out how you will achieve your goals while still fitting into your current lifestyle. It also helps to keep from feeling guilty about not attending every social occasion.

Most people don't start off as heads of corporations with multi-million dollar salaries and vast legions of employees at their beck and call. Most people don't have the luxury to say no to things that aren't a part of some five-year plan. This kind of planning is reserved for those who are already on top.

To take stock of your situation, list every single piece of your life. Don't forget the big stuff – what you do for work, where you live, who you live with, how much money you get a month. Don't forget to include the little stuff: what sports you play; how many pets you've got; your bowling average; etc.

And don't be afraid to write down anything at all – even if it seems insignificant now. It could be important later on when it comes time to make a plan. Once you've listed everything, take stock again. In order to make a good plan, you'll need to add up all the things that are currently missing from your life. This will help you see where you stand at this point in time.

Now that you have a list of everything that's lacking – the things that are not currently happening in your life – there is one question left to answer before we move on: What would it take for me to achieve my goals? This is what we'll be covering in chapter 2.

<u>Excuses: The lies we tell ourselves</u>

"I'm too old to move to a new city/start a new job."

When someone says "I'm too old" it's usually an excuse. This always happens when you reach your mid-thirties and you've finally done all the work that you wanted to do before then. You're not too old, too young, too broke, or too lazy. You're just another half-interested waster of an adult who has some idea of what he wants but doesn't want to do the work necessary to get it.

Excuses are the bane of our lives. They make us feel inadequate, when in reality we're fully competent to handle anything that comes our way. An excuse stops us from learning who we are and what we can do. The thing about excuses is, is that they're usually just a misfiring of the initial desire to do something, coupled with what you've already learned is ok not to do.

But enough about excuses already, let's start by looking at how you get them and why they persist as you age. Things come up in life like paying bills, moving out of your house or a job loss. The reason you've lost this job is because of your boss. The reason you have to move out of your house is because the landlord doesn't keep up the home. The reason you have to pay those bills is because you haven't been taking care of them. You didn't do anything wrong, it's just things come up and you are left flailing around looking for an answer and some way to get through it.

As a result, we turn on our excuses as a kind of trusty old friend who will help us through things most of us wouldn't want to experience again. We lie to ourselves because it makes things easier to deal with on the spot, and that's fine. We can't deal with everything at once.

Excuses are a form of self-preservation, but they're only telling you one side of the story. They don't tell you when things will get better or how to fix them--just that you shouldn't do anything. They don't tell you what to do in the meantime, just that nothing is worth doing for now.

So, here's a rule about excuses: always consider them lies told to yourself by your own negative imagination. Maybe it's true, maybe it's not, but it will always be a little true in your head either way. So don't believe it--don't even consider it. Understand why they persist, and then let them go.

What's your excuse? Why aren't you exercising for two hours every week? Why haven't you started that side business you've been thinking about? Why aren't you practicing your favorite instrument every day? Why have you been lying to your friends and not taking care of your life?

The real problem isn't that you don't want to exercise, it's that you have excuses that make exercising seem like too much work. When it comes to carving out time in your life, exercise is usually the most trivial thing. You can do it with some effort and a little bit of planning. Working an hour every day on your side hustle won't be hard either, but you'll have excuses up the wazoo.

You'll say that you have too much to do at work, or that your friends are no longer interested in what you're doing, or that it doesn't matter because you're not good enough. And then another excuse will come up and then another and then another until eventually exercise and music lessons will seem like a terrifying possibility.

And when it comes down to it, exercise and music lessons aren't going to kill you. They aren't going to obliterate your life with their impossible demands. The only thing they're going to do is make you feel better about yourself in the long run. They're going to give you a sense of accomplishment that's going to spill over and make you feel better about everything else in your life.

The excuses aren't real--they're just the last layer of low-hanging fruit between you and something good. Imagine yourself sitting at a table with a cake in front of you. The cake is big, delicious and totally real. But under it are tons of excuses that keep you from trying to eat it, each one saying, "you don't deserve this." So, you sit there, look at it and think how great it would be to eat that cake instead. Don't think about the cake--think about why you want to eat it in the first place.

There's good out there, but it's hiding under a growing pile of excuses. Don't waste your life on the dead weight that is excuses.

So how do you get rid of them? First, find some way to turn them into something positive and worth doing. Maybe you'd like to start an exercise routine with your friends at work--but why? Or why not start eating healthier? Or maybe you'd like to read more? You need something to do that will make exercise or music lessons seem worth the effort. Otherwise, they'll just be another excuse that stops your progress.

Second, squash them as soon as they show up, whenever you can. When you catch yourself saying "I don't have time to exercise/start a business/play the piano" immediately turn it around and say something like "that's not true, my time is mine and I can do what I want with it." Then get rid of the excuse.

Third, understand how they work and how you developed them. This will give you ammunition in squashing them in the future.

Get a journal and start recording your thoughts. Whenever you have an excuse show up, stop yourself, record it, then attack each excuse one at a time by figuring out how you developed that thought into an actual excuse.

The fundamentals we'll be working on

What areas of our lives will be examined as they relate to our success?

1. Family Life

Parenting, marriage, sex, chores, kids, siblings, parents, and our in-laws all have a huge impact on how successful we are. Most of our excuses come from the comfort zone of our past, which limits the progress we can make in the future. Friends and family don't only give us a reason to live, they also give us a reason to get out and do things that will further us in life. So, we need to take care of our relationships if we expect them to take care of us when it counts.

On those days when all else fails, our relationships can be counted on to help us get back on track. Whether it's a parent or child – your family is there for you.

2. Finances

The only way to do great work is to love what you do". If we aren't focused and driven, the smallest events can cause us to lose focus and drive which leads us to mess up or not even start at all. Without financial security we have no leverage when dealing with other people. People always have an ulterior motive when they want something from you and the best people will only give you what they think you need - if that "something" is money they are not out to help.

We'll go over solid money management strategies, how to reduce our debts and spend smartly. Problems start when we spend money on the wrong things and ignore things that would be important to us. This requires focus and attention to how we spend our money to make sure we are making the best decisions based on our value orientation. Buying a house, a car, or any large purchase requires us to research and weigh options. Financial issues compound over time - if we don't start now, we might be too far behind when we do eventually decide to start.

3. Health & Well-being

Having health is critical for our happiness and success in life. Can you enjoy a vacation when you feel out of shape? Can you enjoy a movie when you are sick and tired? Our health is our "well-being." It affects every aspect of our existence. Without good health, we cannot be happy, we cannot enjoy life's opportunities or challenges, and we can't succeed. We are unable to execute our dreams and goals.

Let us think about why good health is critical for a successful life. To begin with, it gives you the freedom to live a long life. When people feel sick, they often feel restricted from doing things they like to do. They give up on their dreams and don't live freely as they used to before the sickness took hold of them. But with good health, people feel free from sicknesses and can pursue their hopes and fulfill their desires much easier than before. Without good health, people are forced into lifestyles that are less exciting than before when they were well. Friendship and work become dull. In addition, they may give up on their dreams of a better future and even become depressed due to their inability to find good opportunities and fulfill their desires.

Second, we cannot enjoy our daily life as much. When we are healthy, we can enjoy ourselves in our daily activities. We can do things more actively like going for a walk or shopping without feeling worn out later. We don't have to rest all the time because our body is well, so we can take care of other important things besides ourselves like helping our parents raise kids and looking after the house.

What if I'm still not happy?

Will you be happy after attaining financial independence, getting your weight in check, and creating a meaningful life for yourself? Joy is transient. It changes from one day to the next. Our job is not to strive for some permanent state of bliss, but instead to live our lives so that the journey is better than the destination. We can do this by earning more money, losing weight, and making life decisions that will lead us to a better time than we have now.

The fact that progress is slow doesn't mean it's never going to happen. It just means we have to keep moving forward, even if it's slow. If you can make yourself take action every day--even if it's small--that itself will lead you down a road where you enjoy your work and life much more than before.

There's no guarantee that you'll be happy after achieving your financial goals. What's guaranteed is that you won't be happy if you don't at least begin to explore these possibilities.

Your time on Earth is finite, but your potential for human happiness is infinite. If you find yourself unhappy, unhappy for too long or in too many aspects of your life, then it's time to make a change. Some people need to be pushed into taking action and doing whatever it takes to see themselves much happier than they are now. For many other people, however, it just comes naturally from following their bliss and taking action toward pursuing work and relationships that will support them in a meaningful way.

What can I do today to help myself be happier?

Today's exercise is to identify one thing you can do that will make you happy, and one thing you can do that will make someone else happy. Make yourself happy by spending more time working on a hobby or passion, reading a book you're interested in, lifting weights, going for a walk outside or doing anything else that gives your mind some much-needed downtime. Make someone else happy by sending them an email, paying for their coffee, and telling the barista to put it on your tab, inviting them out for lunch or calling and asking how they're doing.

Make it a goal each day to try one new thing that makes you happy and one new thing that makes someone else happy. Be creative with what you do and don't feel like you have to do things just because it's been done before. If this makes you uncomfortable, try giving yourself time limits per day for doing new things. Here are some examples:

- I'll make myself happy by spending an hour working on my hobbies or reading a book I've been interested in for the past 5 years.

- I'll make someone else happy by sending them a friendly email, taking them out for lunch or paying for their coffee.

- I'll make someone else happy by doing something special--like giving them a back massage or doing something so amazing that they tell everyone about it

Anything will give you an excuse to make yourself and/or someone else happy. You have to take action and do these things, but don't feel like you have to do them if it's going to be too much work, or you don't feel like it. Just get started already or find 5 minutes every day that you can stick with this "new habit." If the new thing feels good, then stick with it.

The chains holding you back

What's stopping you from actualizing your dreams? Is it fear of failure? Is it self-limiting beliefs like, "*I don't have enough time?*" It could be worries about money, lack of confidence or past mistakes. Whatever it is, you start with yourself and then can see how your thoughts make your life better or worse.

Why is this important? An unhappy life is a poor excuse for living. It's worth it to take some risk, try something new and see what it can do to your life. If you're looking for magic bullets that will make you happy in your life, then you're in for a long and frustrating journey. If, instead, you take action to be happier and see what happens, then that's the best way to find happiness. If it doesn't work out the way you planned, that's okay. You can learn a lot from trying something new and it gives you new opportunities to be happy in other areas of your life.

CHAPTER 2: THE BIG PICTURE

This is the dream chapter where you'll create a visual representation of where you want to be in life. Of course, you won't actually be able to see your life exactly this way, but you'll use a metaphor to draw a picture that gives you the overall picture of where you want to go.

You'll spend a few minutes here finding something that represents your current life so that it's easier to draw the picture. What type of person do you want to be?

<u>Where you want to be</u>

- Financially

In terms of finances, what type of person do you want to be? If you have no idea, then think about where you want to be in 2- or 3-years time. Do you want to be living in a terraced house, or a detached? Houses in the middle of nowhere or the outskirts of a city? What car would you like to drive? Do you want to be a millionaire or a billionaire?

Is that goal too ambitious? Maybe being just comfortable is how you want to be. So now, focus on that feeling and think of the qualities of someone who's got what they want and has achieved what they've set out to achieve.

Now, take those 2 or 3 key things which are the most important things for you to achieve in your life (Financially). What type of person would need to have those qualities? Take a minute or two and "try on" being someone who's got those qualities. Think about how they might behave in different situations. Think about their habits, thinking processes and character traits.

- Socially

Where you want to be socially? You need a social life that's more than just friends. Is it important to you to have a particular type of partner (or partners) in life? How do you like people and what do you find appealing about them? What are your likes and dislikes about being with other people like yourself? Where do you want to be spiritually, spiritually speaking? If this is new for you, look at this again after a few years as that helps.

Your family and friends are not just important because of what they do, but also because they're who you spend your time with. What sort of person would you like to be around?

- Emotionally

Where do you want to be emotionally? You need to be able agree with yourself how you feel and how you want others to react. Your work ethic, your manners and your attractiveness will all be enhanced by being someone with whom you have a good rapport.

To make the picture more realistic, think of a celebrity, politician or person in media who has what you want, has done what you'd wish to, and is recognized for doing their accomplishments. Imagine that person sitting opposite you at a meal in a fine hotel. How are they dressed? What's their manner like? Are they charming or arrogant? What do they say? Where do they look when they're talking to you and other people in the room? And how does it make you feel when you see them or hear them speak? If it makes you feel insecure, using negative words like "arrogant" might block this out. If it makes you feel excited and inspired, it might help bring your personality more into line with who you want to be.

- Spiritually

Where do you want a spiritual connection? Does your religion or spirituality play a role in how you live your life? If not, then how would it change the way you act if it did? You'll know if this is important for you when the picture comes to life for you. If all this doesn't work for you, then maybe taking up new things or joining something will help. Maybe just going along with something will help. Then decide what things are helpful to do and what things are not helpful.

Your goals should be specific which means you'll have to think about them in more detail than you might have done before. You'll also need to be specific when describing the picture because this raises the energy and makes it more real.

An exercise on visualization

The goal of this exercise is to see the picture you're trying to create in your mind. To do this, you'll have one minute to try and draw it in as detailed a way as possible. You can also try writing down what you see in your mind and putting it down on paper.

For the next exercise, I want you to find an image or picture that works for you. It can be an illustration of something that's happening now, or something that happened when you were younger and was important to you at the time (like a family photo). For example, one person drew their daughter on their birthday with butterflies around her and stars around the sun shining out. Someone else drew their wife, who was pregnant with their first child.

You can then draw on that image or picture and imagine you're there again in that moment. This is a good example from another exercise because if you were there again, what thoughts would be going through your mind? What would you be feeling? How would you act?

Start by finding a picture to work with, then draw a circle round it then choose one of the following images to put in the center of your circle.

- The mansion represents the "haven" in the mind; a place where an individual can be safe and happy. Think of a peaceful place you've been to that's like your haven.

- The road represents the "journey" in the mind: a long and difficult, but also exhilarating journey. Feel like you're on it, but also know that you're almost there. (If you want to pause and reflect, take 2-3 minutes just to stop and think about your journey through life.)

- The mountain represents the "enemy" in the mind: something or someone standing in your way. What you'll need to conquer.

After choosing which image best represents you, write down your feelings, thoughts, and reactions (good or bad).

Let's say that you've chosen the mansion, suggesting that you have a strong need to feel secure and sheltered.

You might write something like:

- I feel like I'm home,

- I feel protected and secure here,

- I am allowing myself to live in my own "safe zone,"

- I feel that I deserve a level of comfort that others don't have.

- My life is going exactly as I want it to.

Without reacting to them, observe your thoughts as you scribble. Be mindful of the images your subconscious is creating - don't react to them, just observe.

As you go through the entire exercise you will likely notice a few patterns emerge. You may realize that you feel a need for:

- Security,

- Touch,

- Acceptance,

- Love, or something else entirely.

If you open up to your intuition and let your subconscious speak to you, this exercise will give you an incredible insight into the way that you are thinking. This can be a really powerful way of getting in touch with your true desires. Taking the time to imagine what it is that truly makes you happy can help bring those things closer to being a reality in your life. Visualizing success is a great exercise for anyone - whether they're looking for inspiration or just some guidance as to where they need to direct their energy and attention.

Success is subjective

What success means to you might be different from what it means to others. When talking about things like satisfaction, happiness and career goals, the answer can be so subjective that the word "success" is lost.

The key to achieving any goal is having a clear picture of it - that's why we're doing these exercises on visualization - so that you can work with your mind to make it a reality.

Start by imagining where you want to be in the future and how you want to feel. Then, you can picture the kind of person you want to be. If there was a cartoon picture of that kind of person, then what would it look like? What would it wear? What would its hair look like? What sort of voice would it have? How would it act in certain situations? And how does that make you feel when you think about that person or even see an image of them in your imagination? Are certain actions more important than others for achieving the goal or feeling satisfied in life?

Your SMART goals

Your SMART goals need to be Specific Measurable Achievable, Realistic and Timely.

- Specific

You should be able to picture, describe or show something when talking about your goal. If you're not able to be specific, then it's probably not realistic for you to achieve it.

- Measurable

You'll know how you're doing with your SMART goal if you come up with actions that can be measured. For example, "I want to take up a new sport" is not measurable but "I'll take up golf and play twice a week" is measurable as we now know how often you'll have to do it.

- Achievable

For a goal to be achievable, it needs to be possible within the time you've set. For example, if you want to lose 5 kilos in three months, then it's likely you'll find the time and resources necessary to achieve the results you have in mind. If that's not the case, then check again whether or not the goals are realistic and whether they're something that can be achieved.

- Realistic

You need to ask yourself whether your goal is as realistic as you think it is. If it can't or isn't real or doesn't make sense, then that may mean that your picture of what success is isn't real either. For example, a person who wants to have their first book published or make a CD or host their own radio show but has no interest in writing or singing. You need to be able to see how what you're trying to do will get you there, otherwise it's not realistic.

- Timely

If you don't know when you want to achieve something by, then it's hard to work towards that goal. Or if you want the results by next week, that's not realistic either. With both the time and date given, it gives the goal focus and helps with motivation because either way, there's a sense of urgency which is important for success.

What areas of your life should you be improving on? Maybe your finances, health, or relationships. Or maybe you just want to be more positive. For each of these areas, we'll need to set SMART goals and work towards them. Here's how we can set SMART goals in each of these areas

Goal 1: I want to get my weight in control

This is a health goal. We can turn it into a SMART goal by asking ourselves the following questions:

- Is it specific?

We can make it specific by saying what kind of weight we're aiming for:

- Is it measurable?

You need to be able to work towards something in terms of a goal. For example, if you want to lose 5 kilos in 3 months, then you need to know how much you will weigh throughout that time. We can make the weight number or target number measurable by measuring the scale or stepping on the bathroom scale at the same time each day or doing a weekly weigh-in.

- Is it achievable?

Will you be able to spend at least two hours at the gym each week? If you can work out for a longer time, will you? Instead of the gym, can you walk for an hour or so each week? Or maybe can you walk with friends or family instead of going to the gym.

- Is it realistic?

We might not be able to achieve this goal if it's something that's not realistic. For example, if we've never been to the gym before and now we're trying to spend three hours there in one day, then that goal may not be realistic because we have no experience with it and have nothing to go on. If you've never been to the gym, then you need to ask yourself whether that's something you really want and whether it'll be realistic.

- Is it time-bound?

If it's not time-bound, then we could put some time limits in place so that we can keep track of our progress. One option is to set deadlines for completing certain tasks: for example, if you want to lose 5 kilos within two months, then each month, the scale should tip by at least two kilos.

A positive environment

After you've created your SMART goals, you need an environment that's going to help you reach them. This means that you need the right support-, motivation- and ethic-building resources. To make it easy for yourself, don't put off working towards your SMART goals because if you do, then it'll be harder to work towards them later on when the time comes. You might find yourself procrastinating as we all do from time to time because of things like work, a busy social life or things that will just distract us from doing what we want to do.

The environment that you're currently in should be helping you meet your goals. Let's say that you want to start a diet. You know what you have to do, you've created SMART goals, but then your fridge is full of takeaways, you've been going out for dinner a lot and so on. Although it might seem like there's not much more you can do in that situation, it's important to remember that this is something to work on. So don't just sit around feeling down because of what's been happening. That may make things worse and then you'll just get stuck in that way of thinking which will stop you getting any help at all. Instead look for support from others who can help you be accountable, find things to motivate yourself with and develop improvement steps that are going to work towards your goal(s).

If you need help, you can find support through the following:

- Your friends and family.

Don't tell them what to do, just ask them to be supportive. If they're not sure how, then ask them what you can do together so that they can help you out. Asking for help is the first step to getting it!

- Professionals

A dietician or counsellor who will guide you towards a healthy way of living and eating. A financial advisor or financial consultant who can help you to check your finances and make sure that you're on course with your goals. A fitness trainer who can help you get fit and set up a gym environment that's going to foster success. A marriage counselor who can help to improve relationships or a psychologist who can help with your self-esteem and focus on your goals.

If you need to, you can even hire professionals to help you. Why don't you try it? It may sound like a luxury but if you're serious about it, then it's a good investment in yourself. After all, if money is the only thing stopping you from hiring someone, then it'll be good for your finances as well! You might think that hiring an accountant is only for big businesses and not for individuals but by doing so, you'll be able to save in the long run and also be able to spend more time doing what really matters to you.

Making the plan

Now you know what it is that you want to do, and you've found the resources that will help you reach your goals, it's time to make a plan! We'll be making three plans, a yearly, a daily and a weekly plan. All the plans will be following the same format and it'll be based on the three steps of goal setting: setting SMART goals, making a plan to reach those goals and making a plan to keep things going once you've reached them.

You'll need to make a rough plan at first which will help you to identify your main needs, resources, and goals. Then as you get more experienced and learn more about yourself, you'll create new plans and change old ones if appropriate.

The yearly plan will be created by answering the following questions:

- What are my SMART goals?

- Who will I ask for help?

- What resources will I use?

Based on your yearly goals, you can start making plans for each month so that you know exactly what you need to do. Once you've made a few monthly plans, then it's time to start working towards those goals using your daily and weekly plans. The daily plan is the easiest to make and it's the one where we'll be checking our progress often. The weekly plan is the most detailed of all and it's the one that will be created at the end of each month so that we can see how we've been progressing. You'll need to fill this in every week, so it gets more work than the daily plan.

You should keep a logbook where you can capture your progress and write down any advice that you might have been given. You can also use your plan to keep you on track throughout the month.

Chapter 3: Our Toolkit

In the last chapter, we discussed how SMART goals help us to reach our targets and we also talked about an environment that will help us reach them. In this chapter, we're going to talk about the different tools you can use to help you as well as your social life. These are things that will work with the tools that you've already created: your SMART goals, environment, and support system, so it's not something that you'll need to create yourself.

We'll be creating a toolkit where we'll have different tools for different problems and challenges. You don't have to carry all of these tools with you at any one time, but it'll be helpful to know that they're there if you need them.

A pomodoro timer

In the '80s, Francesco Cirillo who was a struggling university student developed a simple and effective time-management method that became known as the Pomodoro Technique. As he was studying, he realized that his focus would frequently dissipate after twenty minutes of studying, so he came up with a way to combat this. He set a kitchen timer for 20 minutes and would focus on the task at hand for the full duration. After the 20-minute period had passed he'd then reward himself by taking a five-minute break in which he'd do something fun and not related to his work.

After doing this for some time, Francesco developed four rules that help guide him while using the Pomodoro Technique:

- Work on challenges that can be accomplished during one Pomodoro session.

- Every four Pomodoros reward yourself with a longer break (10 to 20 minutes).

- Avoid distractions and do not interrupt your focus on the task with tangential thoughts.

- Break up the work into increments of 25 minutes to help you stay focused.

What's great about the Pomodoro Technique is that it's simple and it does work: you'll find that when you use this method, you'll be able to stay focused for longer periods of time on the challenges that will help you achieve your goals in life.

A pomodoro timer will also be extremely helpful because it allows you to follow a routine, making sure that you're taking breaks at certain times of the day. You'll notice how much more productive you become as a result of following these same routines every day.

Why did he name it the pomodoro technique though? At that time, Italian chefs used a similar technique to determine the exact amount of time required to make tomato soup. He found out that it took around five minutes for the water to boil, and another twenty for the ingredients to simmer. He found this time to be perfect for him, as the technique worked best when he was in a state of flow, so he decided to name it after this.

You don't need to use a kitchen timer when you're using this method because most smartphones nowadays have a pre-installed timer. One of the most popular apps for Pomodoro technique is called 'Tomato' and it only costs $2.99. There are free ones, paid ones, free websites, and paid websites too.

The 25 minutes work period is arbitrary. If you can work for longer, do so. If you find yourself getting distracted after 25 minutes, then gradually decrease that time period by a minute or two. You'll find the time to be perfect for you.

After every 4 Pomodoro sessions, you should reward yourself. It doesn't matter what kind of reward it is but, you should definitely have one in place. A short walk, calling your significant other to catch up or watching TV for 55 minutes so that you have 5 minutes to get ready for the next session, are all great ways to reward yourself. The key is that these rewards don't interfere with your work.

If you find yourself getting distracted by the Internet, turn off your Wi-Fi or just turn off the Internet on your phone altogether. You can get notifications from websites like Facebook so that you know when something important happens (but don't do this during a break).

Sleep, food, and hydration

The second tool in our productivity toolkit is sleep, food, and hydration. Sleep is a vital part of life but many of us don't get enough of it. In fact, studies have shown that a lot of people will say they're getting more sleep than they really are. Most adults need between 7 and 9 hours of sleep-in order to feel fully energized and focused. So how can you make sure that you're getting the right amount of sleep?

Most people set their clocks to be at a certain time and will then wake up or go to bed at the same time. Our circadian rhythm is slightly longer than 24 hours so as a result, we're going to get tired at a certain time. If you've been setting your clock for 8 or 9 hours like most people do, then you're going to be waking up or falling asleep when your body forces you to (which isn't the right time).

Instead of using the clock on your wall, use an app like Sleep Cycle. It'll allow you to start tracking the quality of your sleep so that you can figure out when your body wants to get up in the morning and what time it wants to go to sleep: start with waking up at 6 in the morning without an alarm and see how sleepy you feel.

Your sleep will improve if you keep your room as dark as possible in the evening. It's best if you don't drink anything after 9 pm and definitely no caffeine. Instead, use an app such as f.lux that will allow you to gradually change the light of your screen to be as dim as possible at nighttime.

Your sleep quality also depends on your diet, so it's best if you make sure to eat a balanced meal that contains proteins, carbs, and healthy fats. It's also very important that you keep yourself hydrated throughout the day because drinking a lot of water will help you sleep better at night.

Positive self-talk

This tool isn't a physical one but it's just as important as the other two. If you want to achieve your goals, then you need to stay positive. You can achieve anything if you stay motivated and determined. The fact of the matter is that whenever you find yourself in a negative situation, it's because you've put yourself there: if someone makes fun of you for a decision that you've made, it's because deep down inside that person doesn't like where they are in life so they're taking it out on someone else.

A lot of times we say things like "I'm not good at math" or "I'm not good with people", when in reality we're just bad at being assertive and getting what we want. If you have a hard time dealing with certain situations, it's best if you take steps to improve your skills.

Instead of playing the victim and blaming the situation, always stay positive. One of the easiest ways to do this is to reply with a question whenever someone says something negative about you.

The other person will be forced to answer your question and that leaves them no time at all to criticize you.

Affirmations are another great way to stay positive. Whenever something goes wrong, you can use an affirmation to turn something negative into something positive: instead of being anxious about negative results, you can be excited about the rewards that are yet to come. It's best if you write down your affirmations on a piece of paper and read them every day.

It's important to keep a positive attitude at all times, especially if you want to achieve your goals.

The problem with bad habits is that they're hard to break. We all have them: from being lazy to procrastinating, from letting our anger take over us to being worried about things we can't control, we've all been guilty of it at some point.

What holds us back from breaking these bad habits is the fear of change. When we're anxious and anxious to try something new because of this fear, we're more likely accept failure and our old habits than try something new out of fear of failure.

A journal

It's been said that if you want to be a writer, you have to write. The same holds true for business: if you want to be successful in these fields, you need to keep a journal. Keeping a journal will help you analyze your life and determine what areas of your life are working as well as which ones aren't.

The entries in your journal don't have to be long or detailed but they do have to be written down. You don't need to publish them, but you do need to read them every now and again so that you can stay motivated and inspired. Your journal is a way to hold yourself accountable. It's a way for you to force yourself to put your ideas down on paper so that you can start becoming more productive. If you're struggling with this, then my advice would be for you to spend 15 minutes every night writing about what you did during the day, the things that went wrong and the things that went right.

When we're feeling down or when we're afraid of something, it's very easy to fall back into our old habits and convince ourselves that we can't do anything about it. It's very easy to convince ourselves that we're too tired, too busy or don't have the skills to take on a new project.

Has this happened to you? Do you sometimes feel overwhelmed by fear? Do you sometimes feel like giving up in the middle of doing something because it's just so hard for you? The best way to deal with this is through a source of motivation. Instead of focusing on how far you still have to go, focus on looking back at how far you've already come.

The journal will keep you motivated as you go through life, and it will give you a glimpse of how far you've already come which helps you realize that this is only the beginning. You want to make sure that every entry gives a glimpse of the person you want to become and the life that's inside your head.

The night before routine

What does your current sleep routine look like? Do you wake up at the same time every day? Do you use the exact same alarm clock for the last few months because it's the only one you've got?

Those are all habits. The moment that we allow ourselves to fall into one of these routines, we've already lost. We've already fallen into a trap.

It's important to create your own routine and stick to it until something new comes along: otherwise, it'll be very easy for habits of self-destructive behavior to sneak up on us without us realizing it. What's even more important is that we're able to see these habits and replace them with something else.

Here are a few examples of self-destructive sleep routines:

1. Binge watching

It's always one more episode before bed, because it's on late and you'll just catch the end (and then the next day, it's another one). But I've turned the lights off for five minutes and I'm not tired... so I'll just watch this show. Then, suddenly, it's 2AM and you're tired – but now you've got to be up at 7AM.

2. Having screens in the bedroom

It's easy to fall into the habit of using your phone while you're sleeping. Both of these are habits and they're not going to help you in the long run: you'll be much better off if you put your phone on silent and turn off the lights. No TV. No computers. No tablets. No smart watches. Just you and your mind at night: all quiet and peaceful, allowing the darkness to do its work and prepare you for the day ahead of you.

3. Late nights

If we turn off our alarms and keep on snoozing every other minute, we end up late for work after half-sleeping for a couple hours before getting up for work.

Decisions on autopilot

Perhaps the most important skill you'll learn from this book is making decisions quickly. It's the one skill you will always carry with you, no matter what happens in your life. If you know how to make good decisions quickly, then you can make a fortune if the market crashes or start a new business if the economy is booming. You can also implement new ideas on the fly if someone else has an idea that could be better than yours and you have to beat them to it.

The problem is that most of us are too slow at making decisions or too hesitant: we're often afraid of making a wrong decision and this fear paralyzes us from action. We become controlled by fear, and we let ourselves believe that we need extra information before we can make a decision.

And in many cases where additional information is not needed, it can actually be a bad idea.

To overcome this paralysis and sharpen your decision skills you must first accept that you have a "decision fatigue" problem and that you're usually afraid of making the wrong choice or being wrong. Once you accept that fact then it will be easier to turn it into an advantage to speed up your decision-making process: we become more confident knowing that we can't be wrong. When we know we can't make a bad choice, then we actually become faster at making decisions because our intuition makes our choices for us so quickly.

Here are the basic steps to make better decisions:

1. Use your intuition to make decisions and quickly implement them. Once you've learned how to do it, you'll feel powerless in your daily life; you'll be able to take action on an idea in minutes rather than hours or days. You will also be able to implement ideas much more easily and quickly, so that you can beat competitors who are slower or hesitate about implementing their ideas.

2. Accept failure, because failure is just a way of learning what not to do in the future. (This is probably the most counter-intuitive habit of all.)

3. Don't be afraid of making decisions: you can't be wrong if you're confident about your decision.

4. If you need more information to make a decision, ask for it quickly or find it on the Internet, but don't procrastinate by always "waiting for more information." Decide on the spot, and then go look for that additional information.

5. Make very short-term decisions: focus on the small task in front of you and decide what to do right now using your intuition.

Chapter 4: Your Time

Productivity isn't measured by how many hours you work but by the quality and quantity of work you get done. However, there are a lot of people who never seem to be able to find enough time for what they want to do. Many people think that time management is about making lists and ticking off boxes; it's not, it's about understanding why you have trouble managing your time and fixing that problem. We'd all like to have more time in the day, and we think it's impossible without giving up something else.

Adulthood is interesting: You have to balance getting in all the things you want to do with making sure that you have time for your other priorities: family, friends, and hobbies. You also have to make sure that your work is keeping up with your life. You can never get more time if you don't get rid of something else. The trick is to go through your list of tasks and find out what activities are taking up too much time and what other activities could be squeezed into the gap. In this chapter. If you want to be more productive, then you need to learn how to say no. You need to learn how to say no, or stop doing something else, but still make progress on your main goals. You could always choose easier goals and do something similar that's less ambitious but learning how to say no is a step towards growing up. The best way to end the day with a feeling of accomplishment is by saying no and setting priorities: focus on what's important and let the rest go.

The hardest part about prioritizing is it can feel like you're choosing between things you want: it feels like everything has equal value. If everything really does have equal value, then it wouldn't be hard to choose. However, in life there are things that are more important than others and if you can't decide between them, then you'll never get anything done. You've got to find out what's the most important thing you want to do right now, and then do that instead of everything else on your list. Then the rest will "evaporate" into nothingness until the next time around: then you'll be able to make a different choice again.

Prioritizing tasks

What do you do when you're required to do three things at once? Most people say that they will just work on them as fast as possible, simply because it's easier to get them done faster than doing one thing at a time. However, this won't necessarily make you any more productive. It's better to take one task at a time, then move on to the next one and finish that as well. If you repeat this process over and over again it will provide you with more satisfaction than if you try to rush through three tasks at once.

The best way to prioritize what tasks require your attention is by writing everything down on a list: most people believe that it is impossible to do everything that they want in their lives, so they avoid making lists. If you don't make a list, then it is harder to prioritize tasks and decide what's most important.

Here's the basic process of prioritizing tasks:

1. Write down all of your tasks, organize them as they appear in your day. Your morning tasks can be at the top – but only if they are most important.

2. Make a rough estimate of how long you will spend on each task.

3. Determine which tasks are the most important and should take precedence over everything else: when deciding which tasks to

leave for later, you should keep in mind what's most interesting to you at that moment. These are your top priorities, then choose the next greatest concern and so on until items 2nd, 3rd, and 4th on your list of priorities (your "next three tasks").

When to-do lists don't work

A to-do list works. It's a tool that shows you what you should be doing at any given time. How many times have you failed to tick off at least one item on your to-do list? Several, I'm sure. Actually, several times. In some situations, you may think that you're really going to get something done because you're very motivated and productive. But as soon as you sit down to work, your motivation will begin to fade, and your energy levels will go down.

Instead of writing down what you want to do when you wake up, write down what you achieved during the day before you go to bed. I call this the man in the mirror method where you revisit what you have achieved during the day and see how much progress you've made. This way, you have to keep reminding yourself that you've done something. Focusing on what's happened will make you much more productive than focusing on what's missing from your to-do list because it keeps your focus on the things that are done rather than what still needs to be done.

When you know that you'll be facing the man in the mirror who will ask you what you've achieved that day, it is more likely that you'll do something. Before you come home from work to go to sleep, ask yourself what you have achieved that day. When you're about to go to sleep, write down the things you have done so far and then you will do something tomorrow before bedtime.

This mindset shift from 'what has to be done" to "what has been done" will help you to be more productive and happier. You'll be grateful for everything you've achieved. At the same time, you'll try to find out what you can do better the next day.

Breaking down projects into tasks

How do you eat an elephant? According to Desmond Tutu, *"you need to break the elephant into small parts."* You need to start with the smallest piece, and you have to take a bite out of it one at a time.

Knowing that your goal is too big can be tempting: it may seem better to try and do something difficult all at once rather than going straight for the goal. This causes procrastination because you don't know how to break your goal into smaller pieces and what's more, you can't even see how each part would fit together because it seems like an impossible task.

Break down your larger tasks into smaller ones – this makes it much easier and helps reduce the feeling of overwhelm by making progress more manageable. By breaking your project into smaller parts, you will be able to see exactly what needs to be done as well as the time it will take. It also makes it easier to find the motivation to move on to the next step because you have something that's already been achieved.

How do babies learn to speak? One word at a time? How do masons build a house? One brick at a time. Each small step is insignificant on its own but in the grand scheme of things, they will amount to something great. Therefore, don't try to take it all on at once: just focus on one step at a time and do your best.

Breaking down projects into tasks

Let's say that you want to renovate your kitchen. There's so much that you'll need to do. You may need to change the plumbing, the carpet, the flooring, the paint, and light fittings, and so on. You'll need to get a kitchen designer, you'll need to change your kitchen cabinets, you'll need to install new appliances, and so on. All these are different tasks in the project of renovating your kitchen.

Breaking down your project into tasks is important if you want to be productive. It makes each task more manageable and compels you to get started immediately. If the task is broken down into smaller steps, it becomes easier to take action and complete the task without procrastination.

You could break down your kitchen renovation project into steps such as:

- Get an estimate for plumber, electrician, and carpenter.
- Buy paint, carpet, and flooring.
- Order kitchen designer's drafts for cabinet design.
- Get kitchen cabinets installed.
- Purchase appliances.
- Apply for electricity connection and water supply.

The more complicated your project is, the more likely you are to procrastinate. But if each task is broken down into smaller steps that can be completed within a day or two, then it makes it easier for you to start taking action immediately without procrastination.

Breaking your project into tasks means that you'll be able to complete each of the tasks in a certain time period and avoid feeling overwhelmed.

As part of breaking down your project into tasks, you need to create a mindset that encourages you to complete each task in a certain time frame. This is called "task-completion mindset".

Take a look at how it works:

Let's say that you want to install new cabinets. You could break this down into steps such as:

- Shop for kitchen cabinets.

- Order kitchen cabinets from the supplier.

- Wait for delivery of kitchen cabinets and installation begins.

- Apply kitchen cabinets to wall and install handles and so on.

- Apply paint, seal off flooring, and change light fixtures

Setting deadlines for yourself

Parkinson's law says that work expands to fit the amount of time you have available. If you give yourself a long time to do something, then the task will seem too big, and it will be hard to even get started. In contrast, if you set a deadline, you will value the time you have available, and get the job done with time to spare.

The idea of breaking your project into tasks is to give yourself a deadline to complete each of the tasks. The beauty of setting deadlines is that it helps you get started immediately because you know that you have a certain amount of time to complete the task. Therefore, it forces you to work on your project immediately rather than putting it off until the last minute before your deadline. You'll be more likely to get started if you set a deadline for each task that needs completing within a certain time span. If one task is delayed, you'll have enough time to complete other tasks as well before the deadline hits.

To avoid missed deadlines, it's wise to find out how much time you'll need to complete each task. Each task may require different amounts of time because some tasks require more research, more careful analysis, more processing of the data and so on.

If you set a deadline for a task that's too long, you are likely to put off working on it. In this case, you would be preoccupied with other activities or tasks that have shorter deadlines and would get frustrated when the long deadline approaches. You might feel like you have to rush at the last minute and miss the deadline again by a few hours or even days. Not only will this make things worse for you in terms of your plans but also your reputation.

Start by listing all the tasks that need to be completed before your deadline. You can do this by writing them down and prioritizing them in order of their importance or urgency. You might need to "prune" certain tasks from the list which you no longer feel are important to complete.

For each task, set a realistic deadline for its completion based on your estimation of how long it will take to complete the task.

Let's say that you need to write a 50-page report to your boss and you know that you could write 10 pages each day on average, so you could set a realistic deadline of 5 days to complete it. This leaves no wiggle room for procrastination as you know that you'll need to work on it every day.

After that, you can set up an Action Plan for each task. In this plan, you outline every step that needs to be completed in order of the priority it has in your list. For our example report, you could start by writing 10 pages on the first day and then go from there.

By writing your Action Plan once a day, it will prevent you from wasting time in procrastinating on your tasks or trying to switch focus to other ones. It will also make it easy for you to prioritize tasks and stick with a strict plan of attack every day without feeling stress or anxiety.

The ever-changing to-do list

Keeping a list of tasks to complete is a good way to manage your life. A list helps you focus on what's important, and what you truly believe you need to do. But a typical to-do list tends to change too frequently, and it is difficult for your brain to keep up with it all.

To keep your to-do list manageable, I suggest keeping it short. The number of tasks shouldn't exceed 10. Keeping a short list encourages you to prioritize tasks and work on only the most important ones before getting distracted with other items on your list.

In addition, if you have a long list of tasks, then you will likely feel overwhelmed and stressed out by the end of each day as you work on all items simultaneously without letting yourself focus on a single task for long enough.

By keeping a short list and prioritizing the most important tasks in that list, you will be able to complete all items in that list with ease before moving onto your next one.

Things will come up and you'll need to adjust your plan as you work on each day and week. But by keeping a short list of tasks, you'll be able to complete them all with confidence, and feel motivated by the progress you've made.

Dividing your day into work periods

When are you most productive? Most people work in the morning and the evening. The afternoon tends to be the period of the day when you get the least done. Dividing your day into work periods will help you take advantage of your natural working rhythms. You'll have more energy in the morning than in the afternoon, and the same goes for evenings.

Let's say that you have these 4 work periods:

- 8AM to 10AM

- 10AM to 12AM

- 2PM to 4PM

- 8PM till late

You could do the most important tasks for the day in the morning and early afternoon, which tend to be more important than the rest of the day. In the evening you can do less important tasks or finish whatever you haven't done during the day.

Relatively speaking, in a typical day there will be fewer important things to do in the afternoon and evening compared with the morning and early afternoon. It makes sense then, to utilize your energy for doing what matters most during this time.

Tasks that involve creativity such as graphic design, writing and programming are best done in the morning. Research, administration, marketing, and general management could be done in the early afternoon when you have energy left over.

Similarly, tasks that require a lot of mental concentration such as reading and reviewing data or researching information about your topic should be completed during the early evening.

If you want to prepare for a presentation or run through some data or figures from your database to test how it would look on paper, these tasks should be completed at the end of each day so that you have enough time to review what you've done and make improvements before your presentation day.

Each work period should be devoted to specific tasks that require the energy and focus you have at that time. By utilizing your work periods wisely you'll be able to increase your productivity by focusing on the most important tasks during each period of the day.

<u>Taking a break</u>

Including breaks into your schedule is essential for maintaining long-term focus and avoiding boredom. By taking short breaks you will be able to refresh your mind, ward off fatigue and avoid burnout.

There are three types of breaks:

Regular – it's a break, which you take regularly during your work. It is meant to refresh your mind and get rid of distraction caused by your work. You can also use regular breaks to do small actions, which do not require a lot of concentration or thinking power. This would include things such as getting a drink, making some coffee, or taking out the trash. I recommend that a regular break should last for 3-5 minutes.

Mini – it's also a break, but between 2 regular ones or just before starting something important. Before you make a presentation showcasing your work, have a mini break.

Tactical– this type of break is needed when you need to slow down and re strategize.

A tactical break is when you take a break to plan your next actions. You need to take a tactical break when working on something complex or with many steps, where you need to come up with an action plan or figure out how to do something once you've finished the rest of your work.

Taking short breaks during the day can help you focus on what's important and refresh your mind. Using breaks will also help you avoid overworking yourself, which can alter your productivity levels drastically in a short amount of time. Taking regular breaks helps avoid fatigue and stress which could hinder your productivity.

Some people have mentioned that taking a break is a sign of weakness and that they prefer if they didn't take any breaks at all. This is counter productive as it means that you are too stressed out having to complete all tasks as fast as possible.

Remember that breaks are a part of your job and taking them doesn't mean you're lazy. Taking regular breaks could actually be motivating for you because it means you'll get more done in the same amount of time. Taking mini breaks allows you to switch from one task to another with ease and pick up where you left off at the end of your break. Tactical breaks allow you to take the time to collect your thoughts and make sure your next steps will be the correct ones.

CHAPTER 5: HABITS

Thinking is taxing. When we think (mentally) we use glucose, but the amount of glucose you need to perform a particular thought depends on how complex it is. Nature loves efficiency. Muscle memory is a phenomenon that allows us to avoid expending brain power on tasks we perform often. The less complex the task (driving vs walking) the easier it is for us to get it done. Similarly, once we are able to perform a more complex task (reading), our brain establishes a neurological shortcut/habit of sorts.

An example will make things easier: Think about how you drive a car. You have eyes on the road, you'll occasional glance at the rearview mirror, your foot is on the gas, you're paying attention to traffic around you, cars around you etc. But how much of that are you actually thinking about? You've done it so many times, your brain has created a "driving autopilot" for your body.

<u>How habits came to be</u>

The same thing happens when we learn to read. Our brain makes a mental shortcut (or "habit") so that from then on reading is simply a matter of performing less complex tasks (sounds like muscle memory). Riding a bicycle is another example. It takes a lot of effort and concentration to learn how to ride a bike—especially the first time. But once we've memorized our "mental map" (how to balance, steer, pedal) it becomes second nature.

Like muscle memory, learning how to read is an example of "neural encoding". We start with complex thoughts and after performing them enough times our brain encodes them as simple ones (and in the process makes a shortcut). That's why kids who haven't learned how to read yet can still speak. They can still store and retrieve words in their mind (ish).

The downside of neural encoding is that you lose access to the information from your long-term memory.

In Neanderthal times, our brains didn't have the capacity to process complex thoughts. Our brain evolved to process only the simplest of thoughts; from this it is reasonable to assume that our body/brain had some sort of neural encoding mechanism set by default.

As we learnt how to speak, our brains started creating easy-to-process and easy-to-remember mental maps (habits) for us. We wrote down these habits on the walls of our caves, in the form of pictures or drawings.

Good habits and bad habits

Fast forward to the 21st century. We are in an age of information overload, and we are overwhelmed by numbers and the vastness of what the world has to offer. A habit may be good or bad; and we can even develop them without knowing.

Positive habits are beneficial to us in the long term, giving us a sense of purpose on a daily basis. Positive habits can include: getting up early, exercising, tidying the house etc.

Negative habits are detrimental to us in the long term, breaking down our brain and causing health problems such as anxiety, depression, or insomnia. Negative habits can include: not eating enough fiber or raw vegetables and not sleeping enough (for example).

A good habit is one that leads us to positive results. A bad habit leads us to negative results.

For example, getting up on time and exercising are good habits which lead us to better health, longer life, and the ability to achieve more in the same amount of time spent working. Now for some bad habits... when we watch too much TV or don't drink enough water our brain gets tired more quickly and we're prone to make more mistakes.

<u>The three phases of a habit</u>

Each habit has three phases: the cue, the routine, and the reward.

- The cue

The cue phase is when we are presented with a trigger which makes us want to perform that habit. The trigger could be a time of day (when you've finished work), or a location (when you arrive home). The stronger the trigger, the stronger it will affect us. If we are presented with a strong trigger, our brain starts looking for a way to satisfy that urge as quickly as possible.

If we aren't able to satisfy our urge at this point, then we'll probably start looking for another distraction until it's satisfied. It's not an effective use of our time as we keep looking for ways to avoid the task at hand by distracting ourselves with meaningless activities.

The longer we resist the urge, the more frustrated we get. Our brain is screaming "do it already" at us. We may even start swearing or blaming other people for our lack of productivity, that's how strong an urge can be.

- The routine

Routine is when you actually perform a specific action that satisfies your urge and helps achieve a goal. Once you do it, your brain will associate the satisfaction with this action, and it decides to use a shortcut next time you are faced with a similar situation (the cue). This means that when you are faced with a similar situation, your brain automatically starts processing the actions necessary to achieve the goal (the routine) and towards the end of this routine it sends you into autopilot.

We've all been in a situation where we've had to do something for the first time, our "brain cog" is moving like crazy as it searches for clues to help us get through this. After we've ticked off step one of our habit's routine (recomposing ourselves), we start working on step two, then three and so on. And after all that work (lots of brain cog activity) we're left with a feeling of accomplishment. We can take that achievement and use it as fuel to keep us motivated.

- The reward

The reward phase is when the habit is actually achieved, and you feel satisfied. This is usually what we're aiming for, the result of the habit. There are several benefits to feeling satisfied or rewarded: you feel happier about yourself, you're more productive, your brain/body gets a break from all that hard work (less stress and fatigue) resulting in being healthier too. And feeling rewarded can do wonders for motivation too: we save up our rewards for special days like good scores on tests or birthdays which in turn make us want to work hard even more.

Let us break down a good habit into a cue, routine, and reward.

Good habit: Exercising every day

The cue

After you get home from work, you take off your shoes and put on your workout clothes and exercise.

The routine

You have a routine you have to go through before you exercise, for example: setting up the equipment, putting on some music or warming up with a few stretches.

The reward

After you finish exercising you feel accomplished. You get to do all the stuff you wanted to do during the day like taking a shower etc. You feel better about yourself and more productive as well as healthier. Remembering all those benefits we talked about earlier will help you stay motivated. You'll want to repeat this process every day because of that feeling of accomplishment after each session.

Good habit: Drinking lots of water

The cue

As soon as you wake up, you drink a glass of water.

The routine

Drink one glass of water after waking up. You could have some fruit or veggies as well or a protein shake. Then go to the bathroom and make sure you pee at least once. After that drink a cup of tea followed by another glass of water and then go to work.

The reward

Having all that water in your body gives you energy and helps keep your skin healthy and hydrated too (if you're worried about aging).

You will feel more productive throughout the day, less stressed and you'll look more professional as well. You'll also enjoy the taste of your water.

Good habit: Writing a gratitude list

The cue

As soon as you get up in the morning, you write down three things you are grateful for.

The routine

You wake up, write down three things you're grateful for and then go for a walk. This could be a walk around the block or just a short walk to the kitchen. During this time, you think about how great it is to have clean water, to be able to read, to hear etc.

The reward

You feel more positive throughout the day and less stressed out as well.

Good habit: Managing your time well

The cue

You start a timer.

The routine

During your day you do the things you have to do like: going to work, shopping etc. After you finish doing these things you decide to reward yourself by doing the thing(s) that make you happy (like watching TV or playing a game). However, before you reward yourself with your entertainment, you have to stop and watch the timer for five minutes. You can't stop it or watch it for any longer than five minutes.

The reward

You get to neglect your work for a few minutes (which feels great), but then you go back to it feeling more energized and motivated.

So, there you have it, a detailed guide to habits coded into our daily lives, one of the reasons why habits are so powerful. And because of that power we must choose them wisely and pick good habits to get us closer to reaching our goals in life!

Bad habits have a cue, routine, and reward just like good habits, but they're not in our best interest. Whereas a good habit rewards you with a positive feeling after performing the routine, a bad habit punishes you with a negative feeling after performing the routine. The cue is what triggers us to respond to the urge and perform the routine which then rewards us if we achieve it. Bad habits have pretty much the same components only we feel bad about ourselves for doing them instead of good. Bad habits can become good habits if you repeat them enough times and associate a positive outcome to them (I'll touch upon this in my next section).

Bad habit: Drinking alcohol after a long day

The cue

You get home from work and feel stressed. You take off your backpack or shoes and pour your favorite glass of wine.

The routine

You start drinking your glass of wine while watching TV or looking at your phone, you start feeling better after a while. After finishing your glass of wine, you feel quite relaxed, so you pour yourself another glass. And as the evening goes on you drink more, maybe two glasses and then some shots with friends. When you wake up in the morning, you have a hangover and feel super stressed out because of it.

The reward

You get a temporary feeling of happiness while you're drinking. You think, "hey I feel better! I'm going to drink some more!" but you don't. You go back to being stressed and upsetting yourself for the next few months, possibly years actually.

Bad habit: Procrastinating

The cue

You have a lot of uncompleted tasks and time is running out.

The routine

You start by browsing through your social media channels, reading the news, and checking your e-mail. You get distracted with a video on YouTube and then you check Facebook for the latest gossip. Eventually you start working, but only for a short period of time. You stop and go back to social media or Google something related to what you were supposed to be working on and spend half an hour doing that. Maybe even longer? When it's finally time to sleep, you feel bad about yourself because you're not productive enough or intelligent enough!

The reward

You feel bad about yourself which means that you're less likely to procrastinate again. Except that doing nothing is addictive and you find yourself procrastinating more, feeling bad about yourself, and making excuses.

Bad habit: Fidgeting

The cue

You're feeling stressed out or you see someone or something that makes you feel embarrassed for any reason.

The routine

You start fidgeting. You don't realize it, but you're constantly doing something with your hands – playing with your finger, twirling your hair, putting on make-up etc. After a while you become more aware of what you're doing and realize that it's not helping relieve the stress. So instead of fidgeting you start talking to someone about the things that make you feel embarrassed about or frustrated about and then some time later it's back to fidgeting again.

The reward

Fidgeting feels good in the beginning but after a while you come to realize that it's not helping. You feel uncomfortable and stressed because of it.

Why is it hard to break a bad habit?

The cue is unfortunately hard to define, but the reward is obvious. The problem with bad habits is that you don't realize you're doing them, but when you do it usually feels good, and you associate the feeling to what you're doing. Because of this reward and your inattention, you'll be willing to repeat the routine even though it doesn't help at all. The problem with bad habits is that they're repetitive – just like good habits – so they become a part of our lives and we eventually find it very difficult to break them because they seem too comfortable or familiar.

This familiarity and comfort make it hard to break the behavior – and harder if you haven't learned to understand why the behavior is a bad habit.

Bad habits develop for a few different reasons:

1) You're imitating another person, or

2) The behavior is emotionally driven, and

3) An action that used to work suddenly stops working, which creates anxiety.

These three reasons are the most common causes for bad habits. For example, when you feel anxious about an upcoming social event (such as a job interview), the anxiety from this situation gets transferred to your body and starts showing up physically in various areas such as your hands sweating or your stomach churning.

Breaking a bad habit

To break a bad habit, we'll need to:

1. Notice the cue

2. Replace the unhealthy routine with a healthy one

To break a bad habit, we need to be aware of the cue that triggers us to behave the way we do. Doing so is the first half of breaking the habit, which is the hardest and takes a lot longer when you're not aware of what's triggering your behavior or why.

Let's say that you want to quit coffee. You wake up feeling tired and groggy. That's your cue to get a cup of coffee. When you wake up, instead, notice your feelings of grogginess and check in with yourself to see if you're truly tired or just bored. You'll discover the cue is not that you're tired but that you're not doing anything.

The second half of breaking a bad habit is finding an alternative routine to replace what you're doing now. Instead of making a cup of coffee when you're bored in the morning, find something else to do to wake yourself up. Do push-ups, stretches and jogging around the block.

Let's see how you can use this habit-breaking strategy to bust your bad habit of using speech fillers in a conversation. The first step to break a bad habit is to become aware of why you're using fillers.

Why do you use fillers? The most common cause for speech fillers is because we start talking before we think. The words seem to come out of our mouths before we know what we want to say. Speech fillers tend to be used when we're nervous about what we're about to say.

To break this habit, you'll need to

1. Notice when you're about to use a filler. You could be in a nervous situation. Notice when you're about to say, "um." This is the cue.

2. Replace this habit of using fillers with one where you think about what you want to say first and then form the words.

Now you might be thinking, "That's too much work!" But think about the benefits of learning to pause for a second and formulate the right sentence instead of letting your mouth run away with you.

Or perhaps you're sitting in class and can't focus on the teacher's lecture. When this happens, realize that it is not because of something wrong with your hair but something wrong with what you're doing. This is your cue to check in with yourself again to see if instead of playing with your hair extensions, there's something else you can be doing that will make the situation better. You'll find that the cause is not playing with your hair extensions but something else that happened before that made you feel stressed out or uncomfortable.

Waking up at night to grab a snack is another bad habit we can break using the above strategy. You wake up at 2am and can't fall back asleep. The first thing you do is head to the kitchen, where you grab a bag of chips. Then you end up lying awake regretting how many calories you ate and how your stomach is rumbling. Maybe you should have eaten a healthier snack instead like a banana or a bowl of oatmeal.

To break your bad habit of waking up at 2am (while others are sleeping) to grab a snack, you'll have to figure out why you're awake. It could be because you're bored, stressed out or in need of a snack. Or maybe it's because you need more sleep. In this case, don't think about what to do to stop the bad habit of grabbing snacks at 2AM but instead look for solutions that make you feel better throughout the day.

Find your trigger and replace it with a new healthy routine. This strategy is the same no matter what your bad habit is, whether it's drinking too much coffee, eating junk food or smoking cigarettes. Break your bad habit by finding what triggers you to behave the way you do and replacing the behavior with something healthier and more productive.

Habit Reversal Therapy

Habit reversal therapy is an ignored method that is effective in breaking bad habits. The whole idea behind habit reversal therapy is that what you do in response to a cued behavior, which is a neutral behavior, controls the cued behavior and replaces the unwanted response.

In addition to managing the unwanted response, habit reversal training is also focused on teaching you how to replace it with a more positive behavior.

Habit reversal therapy shares many similarities with CBT, but the most important aspect of this therapy is that, instead of targeting the thoughts, it focuses on the actions.

If you have a bad habit of biting your nails for example, the cued behavior would be nail biting and neutral behavior would be something else like leg crossing or hand clenching. The trained response will ensure that you're doing one of those two things instead of nail biting.

This therapy is especially useful for people who have strong cravings for a specific habit. This is because it relies on learning the action that will replace the cued behavior.

Once you've replaced a bad habit, you'll be able to manage your emotions without having this unwanted response. With that being said, we should mention that if you have an addictive personality and cannot stop yourself from doing something even after it becomes unhealthy, expect that whatever treatment method you use won't work. Instead of thinking about what's wrong with you and what to do about it, think of why this situation happened in the first place and how to prevent the same thing from happening again.

A Habit and a routine working together

By now, you know that a habit is a combination of behavior, emotion and thoughts that become automatic.

An anxious person may think:

"I hate public speaking. I shouldn't get up in front of everybody."

A person with this thought is likely to develop a habitual response in an attempt to avoid public speaking (by avoiding the situation or by procrastinating). This type of thought may make the person react in a way that is likely to conflict with other things the person wants to happen such as showing leadership skills or being more assertive at work.

The word "habit" is an ancient word that originates from the Latin word habitare, which means "to establish or put in place."

A routine is a series of behaviors that are done regularly, on the same day, at the same time, with similar starting and ending conditions. Your morning routine is a great example. You wake up, get out of bed, wash your face, brush your teeth, have a shower or a bath, get dressed and have breakfast. These are all daily routines that can be called 'habits', but they are also routines.

Routines can also be done in parallel to other behaviors. For example, you could drive to work and listen to the radio at the same time, or you could sit in traffic jams and make phone calls to friends at the same time.

When habits and routines complement each other, they are said to have the potential to form powerful reinforcements. This is because routines that you do regularly and on the same day have the potential to reinforce each other.

This is why you hear people who have a bad habit say things like "damn I need a break from this". This is because when you break your routine for a few days, all of your habits are (partially) disrupted.

It's also why when things go well in life and we feel happy, we tend to reward ourselves with a night out or something special such as going out for dinner with family and friends. We do this because when our routine becomes less stressful and easier to handle, our habits become more effective at reinforcing their own behavior.

Routines reinforce your habits, and your habits reinforce your routines. When either one of them is disrupted, you tend to notice it sooner than later.

Chapter 6: A Routine That Works For You

In the last chapter, we learnt that habits are a combination of behavior, emotion and thoughts that become automatic. We also learnt that habits are part of routines because they reinforce the behavior they are associated with. In this chapter, we'll look at how you can adopt routines that improve your productivity, help you accomplish your goals and most of all help you stay productive.

What's a routine?

Routines are sets of habits that we follow unconsciously. For example, when we get up in the morning, we floss our teeth, we walk to the kitchen and get a cup of coffee or tea, we eat breakfast, and we make our bed. All these behaviors aren't what we consciously chose, they're part of a schema (rule). Eventually, you might stop consciously following them, but they'll still be there in your mind.

This is a sequence of behaviors that we follow unconsciously. Routines have several advantages:

- They save time. By following a routine, you don't have to search for information or think of the best possible solution to a problem. You follow a schema and it's done.

- They reduce the amount of energy or effort required to complete an action.

- They reduce doubt and uncertainty related to performing a task.

- They make sure that nothing important gets missed and everything is carried out properly.

- They give structure to your day, so nothing appears as much of a burden and you're not as stressed out throughout the day.

A daily routine that works for you

When are you most productive? Are you a morning person who's most productive first thing in the morning? Or is the afternoon or evening more your time? Do you have a set time that you work on your goals? Or is it whenever the mood strikes? Do you respond best to frequent deadlines, or would you rather have larger tasks broken down into smaller, similar-sized ones?

Figuring out what works best for you is important when developing a routine that keeps your motivation high and momentum moving forward. If you don't create an effective routine, it's easy to fall off the wagon and not check in on those goals.

The most effective routines are easy to follow and are repeatable at any point in time. Routine can also vary depending on your needs so there isn't necessarily a "one size fits all. If you're currently studying for an exam, your routine will probably be a bit more regimented than if you're interacting with customers for your business.

1. Write down all your daily activities

To create a routine, you need to plan all your daily activities. We'll start by writing down all your daily activities. You will probably have a lot of things going on, but this isn't the time to prioritize or organize them. Just list them down. In case you're feeling stuck, these questions might help you:

- What's the first thing that you do when you wake up?

- Before you leave for work, what do you do?

- What's the immediate activity right after work?

- Take a break? What do you usually do during that time?

- Do you have any hobbies or interests that require special training or classes to stay on top of?

- Do you do anything that requires regular practice or maintenance, like an instrument, car, physical therapy, etc.?

- What are your most important obligations?

- What are your social obligations (family, friends, church, etc.)?

- What do you spend most of your time doing on the Internet?

Now that you have listed all your daily activities, the next step is to analyze them. Why analyze them? We'll need to see if we have any "non-actions" or "idle time."

We want to avoid those and focus on productive activities. Another thing to analyze is what are the time slots when we tend to be more productive and creative? The most important thing to remember during this exercise is not to judge or evaluate any of your activities, just list them down. Ultimately, all your daily tasks are valid no matter how small or trivial they might seem.

If you finish this exercise, you should have a fairly good idea of how you spend your time each day. You can easily spot idle time, non-productive actions, and dead periods of the day when you're less productive.

2. Develop your schedule

Now that we have the list of activities and time slots when you are productive, it's time to organize them into a daily schedule.

There are different methods you can use to structure your day. You can use linear and non-linear approaches:

Linear schedule is a list of all the tasks in chronological order. For example, if you get up at 6 am, then you should have: wake up at 6 am - brush your teeth - eat breakfast - shower and get dressed - etc. If you use a linear schedule, there will be no free time during the day because it has been accounted for already.

A non-linear schedule is when you schedule your daily activities in groups or chunks of time that you consider crucial. For example, you could use the morning to work on your business, exercise in the afternoon and spend evening with family. Instead of listing all your tasks in a day, you can group them into chunks of time and schedule each group separately.

Ultimately, it's up to you which method is better for you. You can use a combination of both methods or even something entirely different.

3. Structure your day

List your morning tasks, midday tasks and evening tasks. Early birds tend to get up at 5:30 am and work all day, while 9-to-5ers may find it quite easy to get away with 8 hours of sleep. The key is to schedule your tasks so you can have plenty of time for non-work activities like exercising, making coffee in the morning, reading a book, or just relaxing on the couch.

Listing down your daily tasks and grouping them into time slots will give you a rough idea of how you should structure your day. You can also use a timer and block out specific hours where you have to take care of them (like working out in the morning). This is crucial if you want to break through procrastination and start being more productive.

Morning tasks are often associated with the most important ones and need to be done first. Mornings, however, can also be some of the toughest times of the day. You're probably not able to focus or prioritize well during this time. In order to get rid of that, schedule your tasks in chunks so they can be accomplished in one go. One way to do this is by using a morning routine that includes some productive activities like reading, writing, and working out.

In the morning, work on the most important tasks first, because of two reasons:

- You start your day with a win – you get things done right away and avoid the risk that you might procrastinate on them.

- You're more focused – your mind is clear and you're not tired yet, so you can use this energy to get things done.

Middays are usually pretty calm and there are fewer distractions. There might be a lot of time slots during the day, but you won't necessarily have to use all of them. You can plan your day so you do important tasks first and schedule less important things during middays or later at night. This is the time to respond to emails, catch up with contacts, do grocery shopping, answer the telephone and other tasks that can be done even if there's not much demand on your time.

Evenings are usually the least productive part of the day because people are relaxed, tired and want to relax. You'll need to schedule yourself accordingly, otherwise you'll run out of time before the end of the day. If you tend to procrastinate at night, then your tasks for this period should be easy and fun – basically anything that gets you motivated so you don't let it slip away. Use this time to plan your next day and get ready for tomorrow.

4. Be flexible

Your routine is probably different every day, so it's important to be flexible. The only exception is your most important tasks that you've already planned. Keeping them flexibly may even help your productivity.

Your Productivity sweet spot

Research shows that there is a peak time of day where people are at their most productive. This is called the "productivity sweet spot" or the "zone of proximal development."

How do we know our productivity sweet spot? One way to find this out is by tracking your time. Get a notebook and mark down your time and activities in different zones of the day.

If you have trouble with time management, there are some apps that help you track your time and show where you spend most of your energy. One of them – RescueTime – also helps you spot if there are certain times where you're less productive. This is useful if, for example, there's a lot of noise around you and it's causing distractions from work. You can tweak the app to set a timer when this happens so that it notifies you and triggers a break from work.

The best way is to track how long it takes for you to finish various tasks. Mark the time for the activities in your notebook or use a timer so you can record how long it took you to do everything. You will realize that there are times when it takes you less time to get stuff done. This is when you'll figure out what part of the day is the most productive.

The best thing you can do to improve your productivity is to start small and scheduled a few things in advance. You will feel more confident when the real work starts as you already have a few things done. If you don't have things done, then don't do them, but try not to stress over work that hasn't been scheduled yet because you won't be able to focus on it anyway.

A winning morning routine

The goal of a winning morning routine is to take control of your day and get you fired up for the rest of it. On top of that, it should motivate you to start a productive day. Start by accomplishing a few easy tasks. These small wins will motivate you and get you in the right mindset to work on more difficult things.

When you wake up, resist the urge to hit the snooze button. Instead, set an alarm for 2-3 hours after you normally wake up (this will be your most productive time of the day). Wake up with a fresh mind, grab a cup of coffee and start reading or writing. You can also use this time to meditate or do some exercise in order to clear your head. Take a break after an hour or two, grab something to eat and get ready for work. In the evening, repeat this process – read or write for a few hours before getting ready for bed again after an hour or two.

Here's an example:

- Wake up at 5:30 am, go for a short walk around the block, brush your teeth and get dressed.

- Don't go back to sleep. Do things that you need to do, like take care of administrative tasks, answer calls and emails and make coffee (you could use pre-made coffee).

- Have breakfast while sitting at the table with the newspaper or don't eat at all if you're not hungry (this will prevent mindless eating).

Your evening routine

After work, you could use the evening to catch up on emails, do research or start working on your side project. You can also work on something that you've been putting off during the day (or other tasks that require more focus than usual). Some people find it hard to stay productive after work, so they stick with their evening routine. They would read or write first and then get ready for bed. Once they fall asleep, they'd wake up at 7:30 am and repeat this process again.

- Have a set bedtime

Working late may be counter productive. A healthy sleep schedule is essential for your mental health. If you routinely wake up at 6:00 am, then at 10:00 pm you'll be more likely to fall asleep without an alarm clock. If you are going to wake up late, make sure that it's not your bedtime too and that you get a minimum of 7-8 hours of sleep every night.

- No electronics before bedtime

Blue light from electronics suppresses the production of melatonin, a hormone that makes you feel sleepy. Try to stop using electronics at least two hours before going to bed. Even if it's something as simple as reading news on your phone or watching a video, keep it under 30 minutes and then put the device away.

- A warm bath before bed

Baths encourage relaxation, which can lead to a deep and refreshing sleep. Use Epsom salts for the bathwater and stay in for about 20 minutes.

- Meditation

Taking a few minutes to sit quietly and clear your head can be very satisfying. It can also help you concentrate better on other tasks throughout the day. Some people find guided meditation works best for them. This is the time to be grateful for everything you have in your life and express any concerns or worries. Appreciate what you have learned and what you have achieved that day. Ground yourself in the present moment and don't worry about the past or the future. Worrying never helped anyone.

- Warm milk before bed

This not only calms your body but also your mind and helps with digestion. The calcium in milk is great for your bones too (if you aren't lactose intolerant). This is another common element of a bedtime routine that works for many people.

- Reading

Reading before bed is a great way to pass the time while relaxing your brain. Some people find reading non-fiction helps them think and problem solve better, while others prefer to read fiction books. Try lying down while you read. It will improve your sleep quality. You could listen to audiobooks instead too.

- Journaling

Write or type about things that bothered you during the day, as well as how you'll solve those problems tomorrow. If there are no problems for you to deal with, write about something that made you happy or caused a positive emotion in your life. Journaling can help with emotional wellbeing and prevent depression.

- Your bedroom is only for sleep (and you know what else)

Your bedroom is the best place to go to when you need to relax. If your bedroom gets cluttered and messy it can be a distraction, so make sure everything is cleaned up before you go to bed. Make sure there are no distractions that could prevent you from being relaxed. Make it as comfortable as possible in your bedroom, so that you're happy in there.

The weekend routine

After a full week at work, it can be great to relax by the weekend. This is the right time to take a short break from work and get some fresh air. The weekend routine should be different from your weekday routine – you're not going to do something productive, instead you're free to go out with friends, play a sport or just relax. If you want to catch up on your reading or writing, this is the best time for it. This is the time to recharge your batteries, so you can come back stronger and more productive on Monday.

- Be social

The social aspect of humans is something that can be easily underestimated. If you value your relationships, the best thing to do is to spend some time with your loved ones at least once a week. The weekend is a great opportunity for this and it's also part of the reason why some successful people take weekends off from work. Go grab drinks with friends. Take your kids to the park. Your spouse will appreciate your time and effort, and you'll feel more fulfilled after the weekend.

Do you play (or watch) sports? This is a great way to challenge yourself, but also bond with friends. Many people consider sports a more interesting way to keep in shape than going the traditional route of lifting weights and hitting the treadmill.

There is an old saying that goes "the best kind of work… is the work that nobody sees." This can be applied to a wide variety of tasks, but just remember that you need personal time to be able to handle the extremely demanding responsibilities you have at work.

Attend work related networking events. These are a great way to mix business and pleasure. If you don't have the time to go out for a meal with coworkers, attend a networking event at work. Your work friends will appreciate the effort and subsequent personal contact.

Spend time with your loved ones. Spending time with your family is important. The weekends are an excellent opportunity to spend time with your family if you don't live under the same roof. Do something fun together such as watching a movie, playing games or go out for dinner.

- Exercise

Some of us don't perform any physical activity at all. It's a shame because there are so many benefits from exercise. It can help you in many ways – it boosts "feel good" hormones, improves your mood, keeps your body healthy and helps you to relax. If you currently don't have time for this, your best bet is to try out a short workout every other day during the weekends.

If you want to increase your productivity, try to set aside some time for exercise every week. Not only does it help you stay in shape, but it's also beneficial for your mental health and overall health. Hiking, running, swimming, dancing, rafting or whatever you enjoy – just make sure it's activity that gets your heart pumping a bit faster.

Working out during the weekends is probably one of the best ways to get in shape. It's not too intense and can easily be done in your free time. You'll feel energized and ready to take on anything when you're ready.

- Read or write

Reading or writing are activities that allow you to switch off from the stresses of everyday life and relax. Whether it's a book or writing an article for your blog, they're skills that will always be useful during your work life. Read the newspaper. Find a magazine that you want to learn more about. Watch a documentary on the internet. Do whatever helps you relax and take your mind off of the daily hustle, even if it's only for a few minutes.

Learn about different topics, even if you're not going to use the knowledge you gain immediately. Reading is a great way to gather information about topics that interest you. Learning something new can make you more successful at work, but it's also an opportunity to expand your mind.

- Take time to plan for the week ahead

You can do this on Friday evening after you get back from work or on Sunday morning when you have time to spare before you go back to work. It's also a good idea to make a short list of your short-term goals, so you can read it out loud and remind yourself what you're working towards each day.

Sunday evenings are great for planning the week ahead. Try to make all the appointments ahead of time, so you won't have to worry about remembering them. If you don't have any appointments, then try to plan a little bit for the week ahead. This can be as simple as making note of a grocery list or preparing some tasks that need to be done during the week, but still get in the habit of planning your life in advance.

- Laundry and the cleaning.

If you don't have a housekeeper, it's important that you spend some time on the weekend to clean and do the laundry so when you get back from work on Monday, your house won't look like a bomb went off. Plan your meals for the upcoming days. If you have time before going back to work, write down some recipes. This is an excellent way to save money and also make healthy food choices that will keep your body fit throughout the week ahead.

"Simple" weekend tasks like meal prepping for the week ahead, doing laundry, grocery shopping and clean up are not only helpful for your physical health but also for your mental health. You'll feel more organized and in control if you start getting rid of the unnecessary things in your life.

You could even use this time to manage your money. Draw a budget. Create a list of your financial goals and important things that need to be done to reach those goals. Review your past month's income and expenses. These are all good healthy habits to develop, even if you don't spend the entire weekend on them.

- Nature

Spending time in nature helps you relax and focus on the bigger picture. Going backpacking, fishing or hiking is an excellent way to help you find your zen and feel refreshed afterwards. If possible, you should try to spend some time outdoors every weekend with a friend or someone special – just make sure it's in a natural environment rather than partying at a club every weekend (though this might be something worth considering as well).

Get out in nature and enjoy yourself.

If there's a park nearby, you could take a walk and enjoy the fresh air.

- Listen to your favorite podcasts

Use this time to catch up on some podcasts that interest you. It's an excellent way to learn something new and keep yourself busy at the same time. You can listen to anything you want, as long as it's something that interests you.

If there's a podcast out there that talks about business related topics, then check it out. Because of this, many mass media outlets have their own podcasts where they talk about politics, economics or sports and tell their own stories from each day of their lives in business.

Podcasts and audiobooks are great because you can listen to them while doing other things. It's sort of like getting a part-time job while doing something else that you enjoy.

- Go on a date

If there's someone special in your life, then it's important to spend some time with them. You can go on a date, or just spend some quality time together at home. This is important for all relationships. Reconnecting as a couple helps you to stay close, which can make your time together even better when you're back home again. Life isn't just about meeting our financial, health and other goals. It's also about enjoying the time we have with those we love.

While many people make more time for social activities and spend their free time at the weekend out in the city with friends, you should consider going out of your way to spend this extra time with your family and loved ones.

- Volunteer

Volunteering is an excellent way to help others. You get a chance to do something for these people that would otherwise not be possible without your help. You can help those who are less fortunate than you through volunteering in a senior or retirement home, or you could even try to volunteer in an elementary school where children can learn from adults who are ready to give back and make a difference in kids' lives.

Teach children about money in an elementary school or day care center. You could also help out at a soup kitchen that provides meals for the homeless. You could do anything you want, as long as it's something that would benefit you and other people.

The job market is a tough game where everyone wants someone who is available to do their work at any time of the day. Free time is one thing you should never take lightly in this world. Everyone needs it to be able to get a good night's sleep, relax and unwind without having to worry about anything else when they are off duty. The weekend is perfect for this.

Chapter 7: Productivity

Productivity is simply getting things done. Productive people get things done, while unproductive people don't.

It's that simple. If your time, focus, and energy are balanced in a way that allows you to accomplish everything that needs to be done without putting in more hours at work than necessary, then you're being productive. If not, then the opposite is true. Productivity isn't about how much work you get done during the work day or work week – it's about how much work you get done and how well it's accomplished.

Being busy doesn't always equal being productive. We're productive when we do the RIGHT things. The things that lead to the things we want to achieve.

Being productive has a lot in common with planning. The reason you are able to accomplish things in a certain amount of time is because you planned ahead and knew what needed to be done beforehand. You thought about how long it would take, how much energy it would require and if it was even important enough to begin with. Productive people plan their days, weeks, and months in advance so they can accomplish everything that needs to be done without putting in more hours at work than necessary – and you should do the same if you want to remain productive during the entire year.

The productivity triangle: balancing Time, Energy and Focus

Productivity is balancing time, energy, and focus. Think about it. If you don't have enough time to finish your work, then you can't be productive. If you don't have enough energy to accomplish this, then you're going to find it pretty hard to finish your work in a satisfactory manner. If you can't focus properly on the task at hand, then the task is going to take longer than necessary and won't be delivered as well as it could have been.

When all three of these things are properly balanced, then you'll be able to remain productive during your work week and get everything that needs to be done finished before the weekend comes around. But if any one of these things starts falling behind, then the others will become much harder to balance as well and productivity will fall behind.

Let's say that you have a project that's due on Monday, which is the busiest day of the week. Your boss comes to you and asks you to put in overtime to finish it by Friday. If you don't plan your time properly and realize that this is going to happen, then there's a good chance that your weekend will be ruined as well because you won't have enough time or energy left over after working on Friday to do all of the things that are important in your personal life.

Even if you don't have a deadline, there are other things that could become an issue. If you want to spend time with your family or do something else on the weekend, then it's important to know in advance and plan ahead for this. If not, then you'll end up having to rush these activities with no energy left over at the end of the week to enjoy them properly.

You can avoid all of these problems if you plan ahead. This way, your schedule is clear for the weekend and there's enough time, energy and focus left over at the end of each work day so that productivity isn't being hindered by any of these things during the week.

Your energy is finite too. If you don't sleep enough, eat properly and exercise, then your energy levels will be down. This means that you won't have the energy to do everything that needs to be finished by the end of the week.

We recharge our batteries every single day. If you don't give yourself the chance to do this, then your energy levels will be low. During the work week, you might be able to get away with burning the candle at both ends and still maintaining a decent level of productivity. But on the weekend when everyone else is relaxing and having fun, if you are too tired to fully enjoy it then it's not going to be much fun for you either.

Energy is all about balance. You have to find a way to recharge your batteries during the week or else stress will get in the way of everything you're trying to accomplish as well as everything that needs to be done over the weekend too.

Our focus is the third part of the triangle. If we have a lot going on in our lives, then our focus is going to be spread out across multiple topics. For example, you might be a parent who works during the week and has kids at home during the weekend. Or maybe you're trying to get into shape and eat healthier at the same time… or perhaps you've got a social routine that you want to stick with but also want to get more work done on your business during the week and weekend as well.

If you are trying to do too much, then your focus will be spread out too thin across these different areas of your life. This could be great for a lot of things, but it's not going to work too well for focusing on the tasks at hand.

Focus is important because you have to be able to give your full and undivided attention to the task at hand if you are going to get things done in a timely and satisfactory manner. Trying to do too much will build stress that affects your ability to focus properly and could lead you into making bad decisions that take longer, require more energy than they need or end up not being as productive as they could have been.

Focusing on one thing means being able to give your full attention to that task, which makes it easier to get it accomplished. It also gives you the energy and focus to do everything else you would like to do in one day as well.

If you need a little bit of extra inspiration, then think back on all of the things that you've had on your "to do" list this week if you're trying to be productive and reach your goals. You might have 5 or 6 things on there that are important enough to be done by the end of the week.

If you had to prioritize them, which ones would be the most important to you? Which would be the most time-consuming? Which ones are going to have the most impact on your life and business once they're finished? You can make these decisions ahead of time and plan accordingly so that you know how much time, energy and focus you'll need during the week… or at least make it easier for yourself to plan for this during the week if you don't have a specific schedule.

Productivity at the workplace

When we're talking about productivity at the workplace, the main thing that we always want to keep in mind is the end goal. The goal is always to get more done in a shorter amount of time. Sometimes this means working longer days. Sometimes this means getting more done in one day than you would have normally gotten accomplished during that amount of time.

If you're not getting more done, then there's not much point in being at your office or working from home… especially if you're expected to put extra hours into your job as part of your employment contract.

To be productive at the workplace, you'll need to

- Eliminate those distractions

It could be anything from the lunchroom to the office kitchen. Or it could be something completely different if your job doesn't actually have any real distractions that are within your line of sight. Whatever it is, the main thing is to make sure that you're sitting down and focused on whatever task or goal you need to achieve by focusing on it so that you don't actually have time for these distractions to take over.

Our phones are another big distraction. It doesn't matter if you have an office or a cubicle. Technology is everywhere these days, so even if you're in an office building with no distractions that are visible to the eye, you're still likely to have your phone on you and there's always a chance that you'll feel like checking your email or playing around on social media... especially if it's not something urgent that needs to be done.

If your phone is too distracting and preventing you from focusing, then consider putting it away for the duration of the day. After all, if it rings or you receive a notification on your phone, then there's going to be a natural urge to check your device.

Emails are another thing that can distract you. If you feel like you're getting a lot of emails and need to respond to them, then try batching them up or replying to them during specific chunks of time throughout the day. This might mean scheduling a 30-minute block of time in the morning where you'll reply to all your emails and then another chunk of time later on in the day.

Block off chunks of time during the day to focus on these tasks instead of trying to check your emails or answer questions while you're in the middle of doing something else.

Don't login to social media while you're working. Well, you can if it's a tool that allows you to continue working, but avoid it otherwise.

- Focus on what is important

Pick 2 or 3 tasks that need to be accomplished today and put all of your energy into completing those goals before moving on to anything else. This will help eliminate any excess stress from having too many things to accomplish, which will allow your focus to be undivided when it really needs it to be.

Instead of trying to multitask and accomplish way more than you should, focus on what you really need to do. Multi-tasking is a myth that's been perpetuated by the media, and it doesn't really exist in reality.

If something else is going on at work during the day, then just move onto that task and focus there for a little bit of time before moving on. That way, you won't be completing any new tasks during your day only to realize that you didn't get anything done in your allotted time that day.

If you're employed, focus on the KPIS (key performance indicators) that you've been given and try to get them done by the end of the day. Give yourself a finite amount of time and then aim to accomplish those things by that point.

If you're self-employed, then focus on getting the most important tasks out of the way so that you can get paid and make money instead of spending hours on something that's not going to benefit your business, like answering emails or helping others while they're working.

- Practice foresight as much as possible

When you're looking ahead of time and thinking about what needs to be done, it's important to put yourself in situations where you know exactly what needs to be done. It's always a good idea to have an idea of how much time each task will take. Plan for those tasks and put yourself in the position where you know that you'll be able to finish them by the end of the day or week.

Situations like these are important because it can help give you a sense of momentum if everything else is done at the same time. If you're having trouble with something, then consider what needs to be done in order to prepare for it, such as scheduling and getting things out of your way so that you have nothing left to do but actually get those things done. This can really help keep your focus on the task at hand instead of other tasks that might take up more time or distract you from what needs to be done.

Your schedule is key to your productivity. There are many different ways that you can go about setting your schedule and the main idea here is to find what works for you and stick with it. Schedule your day so that you have time to relax at the end of the day. You'll want to be able to decompress and go home knowing that you got as much done as you possibly could in one day. It doesn't matter how long your days are or how much time you spend working, just as long as everything is completed by the end of it.

- Take breaks when you need to

Don't try to be a hero. Have a few scheduled breaks throughout your day to help you destress and relax. If it's not because of stress, then you should take breaks because it's important to take mental breaks from the tasks that you're doing.

Taking a break can be as simple as getting up for a few minutes, maybe walking around the office or getting a cup of coffee. It could be something more complicated like taking a short nap or going for a walk outside. Whatever it is, make sure that your mind is clear and refreshed before getting back at work again.

Hydrate throughout the day and make sure you aren't working for too long without a break. It'll be easy to forget when you should take a break if you're in the middle of something, so keep an eye on your time management tools or schedule and make sure that you take breaks every couple of hours or for a few minutes at least.

Breaks are important, but it's vital that you remember to take them before they become long breaks. That way, when your brain is clear and you're ready to get back at work again, it won't be taking several minutes just to get back into their work zone.

- Start with the hardest task

In Brian Tracy's book, "*Eat the frog!*", he suggests that you start with the hardest thing you need to do and then work your way down the list of to-dos. This is important because it can help get a sense of momentum and accomplishment if you're able to check off certain tasks as opposed to moving from one task to another without ever checking anything off.

If there's a task that needs more attention, like something you've been putting off for a while, then it might be better for you to start out with that task and move on after that. Sometimes it makes sense to just start at the top of your list and do whatever comes next, but it really depends on your workflow and how well things get done when they're in a specific order.

Logically speaking, the hard and most important thing to do first is going to be the easiest and most important thing to finish, so it can work against you if you start with something that's not a priority.

- Work in small bites instead of one big chunk of time

If you're working on a larger project, then it might be best to break it up into smaller tasks. When we're talking about a project as large as writing a book or designing an entire website, then you're going to have multiple sub-tasks that need attention. Be realistic about what needs to be accomplished within each task and work your way down the list of tasks until everything is completed.

Break down each project into smaller tasks so that you're not only doing one big task, but a bunch of them. If you were to do it all in one chunk of time, then chances are that you'll give up before getting through the whole thing. If you take it on and break it down into smaller chunks, then you can feel accomplished with each step that you complete and not feel as if something is left incomplete at the end of the day.

As you check off each task, you'll see that the project is slowly coming together, and you'll have much more motivation to finish it than if you were doing one large task in one sitting. Small bites are better than one big bite because it gives your brain a break from the larger tasks of the day and when you're working on a project, it's important to be able to take a break in between each task.

When each task is completed, then take some time off from that project and come back to get it done later when you need to start working on those smaller sub-tasks again.

Productivity when working from home

The Work from Home (WFH) culture has been around for a while, but it's recently been gaining some traction especially in the last few years. With the internet becoming so much more popular and affordable, there has been a boom in businesses operating remotely and dealing with clients who want to deal with you online.

The good thing about working from home is that you're able to control and define your own schedule. There are many people out there that work from home nine or ten hours a day because that's all they need to be productive by; however, with this type of schedule, it's very easy to get distracted from what you need to do so it can take longer than expected for something to get done.

Be honest with yourself about how much productivity you're actually getting done and don't let yourself fool yourself into thinking that you're being productive when you're not. You might be busy, but that doesn't mean that you're actually being productive in each and every task you've done. How can we be productive if we're wasting time doing something that isn't important? To be productive, we'll need to:

- Prioritize everything so that you know what's most important

It's easy to think we're being productive if all we're doing is going from one site or program to another and switching tasks every few minutes; however, if we're not working on anything that's important, then it doesn't matter how much time we "saved" with our multitasking skills. By starting our day with a clear view on what needs to be done, then we can find time for the important tasks and work on them first before moving onto the rest.

We might not like doing some of the tasks that are on our list, but if they need to be done, then it doesn't make sense to not do them just because they're not exciting or fun. What will end up happening is that we'll procrastinate until we're forced to do it and then it becomes a chore and something we dread doing. It's much better off if you schedule in your unenjoyable tasks during your most productive times like right after lunch or right before you leave work for the day.

- Let the people around you know that you're working from home

The people you share your working space with - your children, your spouse, your roommates or even your cat - can really get on your nerves over the course of a day and a lot of the time it's because they're distracting you from your work. It's important to let people know that you need a quiet working space and that you need to focus when you're doing this type of work so that they'll respect your no-distractions policy.

When we get distracted by other people, it often causes us to wonder what they're doing or not do our own work as well as cause us to procrastinate on what we have to do.

Set ground rules with the people you share your space with so that you won't be distracted, but also because it will give you some time to yourself to work when you need quiet. If your family and pets are suddenly in a rush to get outside or inside, then tell them that they can come back when they're done, and they'll be less likely to distract you.

If your space is shared with others, then it's important to let them know that it's not only for your benefit, but for theirs as well. It's good because if someone needs something from you while on the computer, then having a policy of "no distractions" will allow them to go ahead and get what they need with minimal interaction between the two of you.

- Have a home office

If you can, don't work from the bedroom. When you're working from home and have a home office, this gives you a dedicated space that's well-sealed where you can be completely focused on your work without having to worry about what the kids are doing or if the other roommates are too loud. If you have a home office, then it's important to have it for productivity purposes and because it's such an important piece of equipment for working from home. You'll be able to do your best work here and not waste time getting distracted by watching TV or the family while they're all in their bedrooms just down the hall.

Your home office should not just be a work station that you use when you're working from home. It's important to have it as a "work space" as well where you can have all of your work necessities.

- Declutter your workspace.

There's a reason why the saying "no clutter" is one you'll hear your grandmother, mom, and most of the people you know use. It's because clutter can distract you from what's important and make it difficult to get those larger tasks done. Clutter can often be an eyesore and while it may not bother other people that much - especially if they're not as OCD as you are - it can cause you to lose focus and also take away from some of your precious productivity time.

Don't even think about working when all of the clutter hinders your productivity, so start clearing things out to make room for what really needs to be done today.

Clutter in the work space can be as much of a distraction as clutter in the living space because not only is it an eyesore, but it also distracts us from what we need to be doing. It's not just yours either, but also your co-workers, so don't think that you can slack on clearing things up because it will make them liable to do the same or worse.

This goes for all home offices and working spaces, even if it's just for one person who works from home, so tackle those piles and stacks now!

- Get out of the house once in a while

Go work at a nearby Starbucks when your schedule allows it. It might be nice to be in your own home, but if you're going to be working from home for longer than just today or tomorrow, then you'll probably benefit from not being stuck in the house all day long.

Break the monotony of working from home by going to a nearby coffee shop, library or other public space and working there for an hour or two. You'll not only get some air, but you'll also be able to shift your focus onto something else for a while.

A break from your home office is good for you and even if you work from home one day a week, then still get out of the house as much as possible. Having that change in environment can give you a boost when you're feeling tired and make it easier to get those last-minute tasks done so that you can leave the house with a clear mind. Don't underestimate the power of getting away from your workspace after a while.

- Make use of those tools like Google Docs or Evernote

Google Docs or Evernote are great for making notes, keeping track of where you left off at on each task and also to store all of your files so that they'll be available anywhere at any time. Productivity tools like these can really help you become more productive. In Trello, you can create boards for your work area or workspace to keep track of what needs to be completed for each project.

- Leave notes for yourself

Don't underestimate the power of a sticky note. If you're having trouble remembering what you're supposed to be working on, then leave yourself a note! Stick a sticky note somewhere near your work space or keyboard and leave it there until you finish what you need to do for that time period. Not only will this remind you of what's going on, but it can also give your mind something else to think about if it starts getting distracted by other things around the house and office.

A sticky note can be your to do list, you could write mantras on them such as "don't think about it", "don't obsess" and so on. When you have things like this around, then the only thing you'll be obsessed over will be those items that need to be accomplished. There are lots of ways you can use a sticky note, it's just a matter of thinking outside of the box and not letting yourself get distracted by other things in your workspace.

- Set work hours and stick to them

When you take care of yourself, then it becomes easier to focus on what needs to be done. When you sleep well at night, eat good food and drink enough water, then your mind will be clear, and you'll have better energy throughout the day for working from home. These things alone may not make or break your productivity levels, but they can definitely help improve them considerably.

Create a schedule and stick to it. It will allow you to make better decisions and can even help you do more work in shorter amounts of time.

Applying The Pareto principle

Vilfredo Pareto, a 20th century economist, observed the notion that 80% of one's output or results come from 20% of the causes. It's also a principle that can be applied to our lives and work. By focusing on the 20% of the tasks that will get us 80% of the results, then you'll be able to work smarter and accomplish more in fewer time than it takes for people who don't. If a person has a hard time getting his or her tasks done, then this principle can help make that easier.

It's rather simple, when you get home from work or school and have a long list of things to get done, think about what you really need to do and what can be put off for later. Doing so will allow you to focus on the tasks that are important or urgent and in the end it will help save time.

This is just one way that you can quickly boost your productivity levels. You can use this principle for anything: working on a project within an organization, family chores around the house or even for doing homework at school.

Tweaking our routine based on our mistakes and successes

After implementing a productivity technique for a few days, we might realize that it's not working as well as we had hoped. Or perhaps something else has come up and we need to change the way that we are doing things.

You may realize that you had underestimated the amount of time that a task would take, or perhaps you overestimated how much you could get done in one time period.

When this happens, then it's important to go back to what we know works and tweak things from there. If something isn't working out so well anymore, then don't just keep at it and force yourself to do what you're doing, especially if it's not helping your productivity levels at all.

Learn from your mistakes and successes. Think about what changes you can make to improve the way you work from home or work in general.

Observe what's working and what isn't. If something isn't working, then you can try tweaking it a bit or simply ignore it and look for another approach that will work for you better.

Ultimately, the only thing you should judge your productivity levels by is whether or not you are getting the results that you need.

If something isn't working, then rather than beating yourself up over it and trying to force yourself to do what doesn't work anymore, just change the way that you are doing things and make sure that your plan works now. It's easy to get frustrated over something when we have put so much into it only to have our efforts still show no results after a few days.

Accountability plays a big part in our productivity levels. If you are accountable to someone else, then it might motivate you to get things done sooner rather than later. This might be especially helpful if you have a family or friend who is depending on you to get something done, or if you are working on something that requires a deadline.

Keep track of what you accomplish each day in a journal or planner. Take note of how your days went and what tasks took the longest to complete. If there was anything that didn't work for you, then make note of it so that next time if it happens again, then you can be ready to change things up a bit by doing something different from the start.

The more successful that we are, the higher our productivity levels tend to be. In order to become more productive, then you have to make time for making progress. That doesn't mean that you have to do everything yourself by yourself, but it does mean that you have to allow yourself the time and space to make things happen from your end.

If something is getting done or progressing, then make sure that you take the time to appreciate how things are going and celebrate the small steps. Celebrating your successes will go a long way in keeping them going as well as helping you achieve more when it comes down to it.

The multitasking myth

There's a lot of pressure associated with multitasking. Many people believe that if they can do more things at once and during the same time period, then they are ahead of the game. However, this isn't true at all. By over-extending yourself and trying to do too many things at once, you are going to end up causing yourself stress and not getting any additional work done. In other words, you'll be working harder but not working smarter.

You'll be wasting time and effort trying to do too many things at once. It will take you longer to complete everything and your productivity levels will suffer because of it.

The reality is that multitasking just doesn't work. When we try to do multiple things at once, our mind becomes confused about what we really need to get done and for how long we should focus on each one.

We spread ourselves too thin by trying to do too much at once. There are several ways that we can solve this problem, however.

If you have four things you need to get done, then focus on one of them and when it's done, move onto the next one. Doing this will allow you to get everything done without being stressed out about having so many things to do at once or running out of time before getting everything done.

- Multitasking causes burn out

Burn out occurs when you get emotionally exhausted after working for a long period of time. You get tired, and you feel like giving up or simply stop caring about your goals. When we try to do a lot of things at once, we get overwhelmed and emotionally overloaded.

Have you ever noticed how you can be so focused on a certain task that you get 'in the zone' but then you start to get angry and frustrated when another task is brought up? This happens when we try to do more things at once. Our mind switches attention and we start to get overwhelmed. Furthermore, the way that our brain processes information is much different when it's in the routine of completing a single task over and over again versus completing multiple tasks at once. Information is processed differently when it's spread out evenly instead of as a series of bursts all throughout the day. In other words, multitasking quickly becomes impractical for most people.

- Multitasking causes stress

When we're trying to do too many things at once, then we end up becoming overwhelmed and stressed out. We feel pressured when we feel like there's a lot of work to do, which can lead us to make mistakes in some areas or rush through everything else just so we can feel like we accomplished something.

However, not everything that we need to get done is worth burning out over. Instead of doing too much, it's healthier to focus on the things that absolutely need to be done right away and then knock out everything else once you've got the important stuff handled.

If you're constantly switching between tasks, then it will take you longer to complete them and, in most cases, you won't be able to get as much done overall.

- Multitasking causes confusion

We feel confused when we switch between tasks because our brain doesn't know which task we should be focused on or where we should be focusing our attention. Another way that multitasking hurts us is that it takes up more time. When we're constantly jumping around between one task and the next, then it makes our day go by slower than it actually should. However, this doesn't mean that we should avoid all distractions when we're trying to accomplish something. If there is something important that has come up and it needs to be taken care of right away, then it's best to handle it quickly so you can move on with your original plans.

- Multitasking lowers productivity

Even if we can get everything done in a timely manner, multitasking will still hurt our productivity. The way that our brain processes information is different when we're trying to do several things at once versus completing one task for an extended period of time.

In other words, multitasking causes us to compromise not only how much work that is completed, but how well it's completed as well. It's easy to say that doing several things at once can lead to getting a lot more done during the same time frame and while this is true, most people end up sacrificing the quality of their work over the quantity because they are constantly switching between tasks instead of staying focused on them for an extended period of time.

- We're not taking advantage of momentum

When we're constantly switching between tasks, then our productivity tends to slow down because we aren't taking advantage of any momentum that we might have built up in the beginning of the day. Maybe we had a good streak of work done earlier in the day and since then, it's been slowing down. However, catching up with ourselves and finishing off what was left at the end of the day is almost impossible because there's always something important that comes up. Instead, by allowing ourselves to consistently carry out one task at a time and only focusing on that one thing for as long as it takes to get it done, then our focus is better, and our productivity can increase.

In the beginning of this chapter, we learnt that productivity is about balancing our time, effort, and energy. Multitasking is a huge impediment in this equation because it causes us to invest more time in tasks that are not part of our main goals. We become distracted by these unimportant tasks, which lower our productivity and ability to fully focus on what we're trying to accomplish.

It's important to realize that multitasking is bad for productivity because we will always be trying to organize ourselves and do several things at once. This means that we won't be able to get as much done as we could have done if we would have focused on one thing at a time until it was completed.

CHAPTER 8: PROCRASTINATION

At some point, we've all procrastinated at one time or another. In fact, it's almost impossible to completely avoid procrastination because it's a part of human nature. It takes discipline to complete everything that we set out to do, but even then, there are always going to be times where we have trouble getting started.

Why do we even procrastinate? Is it because we're lazy? Could be because we're not (yet) convinced that it's worth doing? Is it because we don't know how to get started? Or is it just because we're indecisive and can't decide on anything in particular?

<u>We don't procrastinate because we're lazy</u>

As we all know, procrastination is really not something to be ashamed of. It's just a natural part of the human species, and nobody ever died from it. We wear our emotions on our sleeves, but if we're honest with ourselves we will admit that our emotions are often one-sided, i.e., "my emotions were out-of-control!"

The thing is, when we procrastinate it doesn't necessarily mean that we don't want to do something in particular. We just lack the initial energy to start something. This is usually because we've just taken on too much, because the task of completing something new is more important to us than what we have on our agenda at the moment, or simply because of a lack of self-esteem.

- We procrastinate because there's too much time

Can you remember what we leant about Parkinson's law? This is the scientific principle that basically says that "work expands to fill the time available for its completion". In other words, if you give yourself more time to complete a project you will find it easier to do so when it comes to the deadline. On the other hand, if the deadline is set earlier than intended you will find yourself struggling to get things done.

Chronic procrastinators know that they always turn into workhorses a few days (or hours) before the deadline, only to turn back into slackers just after deadline. Tasks that take heavy mental efforts to complete are more prone to this type of procrastination, because our minds are always working on bigger, more important projects.

So, should we set deadlines for ourselves that are too early, or should we not set them at all? This depends on several factors, but in general it's better to be careful and not to rush through anything. Timing is critical when it comes to setting the deadline of a project because you always risk ending up with an incomplete product. So, on average and following this rule, if you need more time to complete something it's better to reduce the timescale of the project instead of postponing it for another day or two.

- We procrastinate because we don't have the motivation

Motivation is a necessary condition for all types of action, and yet we often lack it when it's needed. Sometimes things boil down to what we call "energy depletion". We start doing something and then feel too tired / lazy / or too busy trying to start something new which we've put on hold in order to get started on something else.

The thing is, for us to start doing something new, we often need a burst of energy. It doesn't have to be a good one either, as long as it's strong enough to get our attention. Another type of motivation comes from seeing other people's success and wanting to achieve the same.

Motivation is usually both necessary and sufficient for starting things. It can be procrastination that comes into play at some later stage (for example when we're too tired or lazy), but in the end it boils down to the fact that we lack the initial motivation which would lead us to actually get going.

- We're perfectionists

Book authors want to start their book with the "perfect" first page. Accountants want to have all details before making a decision. Entrepreneurs want to know what their competition has in terms of sales figures, etc. Most things we do have an underlying perfectionist attitude, and it's usually difficult to start something new if there are too many details that need to be kept in mind at the same time. We want to get it right all the way through, so we want to make sure that our first step is as successful as possible.

Perfectionism prevents acting and thinking in an impulsive or a spontaneous manner. It's not only hard to start something new when you're a perfectionist, but it's also very hard to complete things with a perfectionist attitude because you never want to let go of anything.

Adopting a belief that "good enough is good enough" can help you get going with things. When you take this mindset, you will be more likely to start and complete things that matter to you.

I'm not encouraging mediocrity. I'm encouraging you to complete things "in a first attempt" kind of way because as long as you know what's important to you, you'll be able to repeat the same action in a better and improved way at some later stage. Just start: You'll figure out the rest along the way.

- We procrastinate because we don't know how to start

Our mental machines are constantly busy, so when we actually want to get started on something new, we need to come up with a plan of action. This is what psychologists call introspection time, i.e., "how do I start this?"

We can procrastinate if the problem seems too big because we don't know where or which part to start with. Or sometimes it's just that we don't know how to proceed because the way to complete things is unclear or indeterminate (i.e., "I have no idea how to start!").

The human brain tends to put off things and avoid doing anything difficult when we don't have appropriate tools to look after the task at hand. In the end, we often don't know what to do even if we have all the required knowledge and articles in our hands.

If you feel that a particular task requires too much effort, then you might find yourself procrastinating because your brain is busy processing information on what needs to be done next instead of starting immediately.

Willpower or discipline?

Discipline and willpower can both be used to combat procrastination. They work in different ways though. Willpower is what you accomplish tasks because you're motivated and that you feel like it. Discipline, on the other hand, is a mindset based on doing things that we don't particularly enjoy because they need to be done. Willpower is a limited resource. It runs out, and it requires too much effort in order to be used again. Discipline is less effortful because it comes from within, and it doesn't require a lot of willpower in order to get you going with the task at hand.

Willpower relies on motivation: Motivation will wax and wane depending on how your day was, who you met, whether you did your exercise today and a zillion other variables. Discipline, on the other hand, doesn't require anything from you in order to work.

Instead of relying on willpower, which is a limited resource, you can simply adopt a discipline which doesn't rely on willpower at all. It's more internal than that and comes from within, from your newfound determination to start the task at hand. You'll sustain this discipline if you apply it consistently for a long enough period of time. Discipline will be easy to maintain because it doesn't require willpower in order to function. In the end, when you want something badly enough and you want to do it more than anything else, then you just work on it "in spite of everything."

Discipline means establishing and sticking to a set of rules that you'll use every time you need to start something. It requires some internal strength, but it doesn't require much willpower. The thing is, discipline comes from within, so all you need is just to find your way to be disciplined: to use a discipline which will work for you by sticking with it until the end.

The 10 minutes trick

This is an interesting technique to beating procrastination. The goal of this 'trick' is to get us started on a task. It doesn't matter what's that task, and it doesn't matter even what type of task it is. The idea is to get us started!

Here's how it works:

1. Pick a task you want to start.

It doesn't matter what kind of task you want to achieve. It could be to learn JavaScript to strengthen your guitar playing skills, or to learn how to improve your earnings with Affiliate Marketing.

2. Eliminate all the distractions

Put your phone on silent. Turn off the Wi-Fi if you're on a laptop. Turn off your internet connection if you're using a computer or a phone. Close Facebook, LinkedIn, Twitter and all the other social networks. Turn off the notifications so you don't get distracted by anything else. Plan to work continuously for that particular period of time no matter what kind of interruption might happen at any moment in time (e.g., phone rings, someone calls you on Skype, etc.). You will be focusing on the task at hand no matter what!

3. 'Lie' to yourself that you'll only work on this task for ten minutes

This is important. Make the time commitment small enough so that you'll feel comfortable doing it. (If you committed to working for "two hours", then this might intimidate you too much and might get you into a state of procrastination!) Just start! Stop talking to yourself and just start working on it! You don't need to spend a lot of time thinking about how you're going to start, just do it already.

Something magical will happen at the 10-minute mark. Your brain will have already switched to 'working' mode. You will be in rhythm. It will feel so natural to continue working. You will get inspired. This is the momentum that you need! After ten minutes of work, you'll be on a roll, and you'll want to continue working. What you thought might be a trivial task that shouldn't take more than 10 minutes in reality ends up taking an hour!

Do you remember what I said about Isaac Newton and momentum? The first law of motion states that "an object at rest will stay at rest unless an external force is applied." Do you know what happens once it's in motion? It will keep going at the same speed unless another external force is applied to slow it down.

Yes, because you started work on a task, your brain will keep working on it even after ten minutes! In the same way, when you work on something for a while, it becomes easier and easier to keep working. This is the power of momentum! Turn this to your advantage!

If you can get started, then you'll only need to invest ten minutes of your time into working on it. Tell yourself that all you have to do is start and worry about the rest later. Say to yourself: "I'll worry about X later." You'll notice that this method is more effective than trying to convince yourself that you should work on the project for two hours.

Another benefit of starting work on a task is that if you start without planning ahead, then this will force yourself to improvise and use some creativity. If you plan everything in detail before you start, then this will take away this pressure and any 'excitement' of getting started will be gone. So, starting without a plan is a lot more fun!

There's a saying that goes: "The devil is in the details." Don't worry about the details before you even get started. You might realize that there are some details that need to change, but this will only become apparent after you have some progress on your project. This also applies to work tasks such as preparation for interviews or sales pitches/presentations.

Analysis paralysis

This might be the culprit behind your procrastination. Analysis paralysis or decision paralysis is when there's a lot of analysis involved when you're trying to make a decision.

For example, when you want to start something and you're thinking about the best way to do it, then your mind gets stuck on this decision. You might also be wondering how long it will take before you reach your goal. Or you might be wondering what the best time is to start working on it (e.g., at night, in the morning, at lunch time).

Sometimes there are too many possible options, and this can make us feel anxious because we're worried that we'll choose the wrong one. We start worrying that other options might be better than what we've chosen. We start looking for different opinions and comparing them in our heads.

We procrastinate by delaying the decision-making process. Often, we don't actually decide on doing anything.

A classic example of analysis paralysis causing procrastination is when you're sitting in front of your computer, and you have 8 tasks that need to be done. You're just sitting there thinking about the different options and not really doing anything.

The longer you sit there, the more you get tired and tired and add more things on your list. You can't get started because you feel too tired to make the first move. You might even ask yourself if you're still in your desired state of mind to do anything that day.

You might start thinking of other things that could distract you from your goal and make you procrastinate even more. For example, wondering what other people think about your project or people who will benefit from it (e.g., how does this project affect my relationship with my boss, school, or co-workers?).

Instead of focusing on the tasks at hand, your mind wanders off and thinks about other things.

- Fill your to do list with easy tasks

Every time you check off a task, you get a feel-good feeling. This makes you more motivated to do more. Dopamine is released into your brain which makes you feel happy. If you write it down, it's easier to focus on these tasks. If you make goals, this will give you a sense of accomplishment. If your list is too long, you might think that the task at hand is difficult and so you procrastinate. It's better to split your tasks into smaller chunks that are easier to achieve.

Start with the easiest tasks first. This way you can cross off a few anyway and it will give you the motivation to keep going through your list of tasks. You'll feel like you're getting closer to achieving something and this will motivate you further.

Simple tasks include anything that you know how to do. You don't need to sit there and think about it. You can work faster on this kind of tasks as well.

- Rewards and incentives work wonders

Set a reward such as "I will not use the internet before I have finished my task for the day" or "When I finish this, I will treat myself to a smoothie." Rewards and incentives work well for simple tasks.

Punishments are just as effective. For example, you might set a rule for yourself "No internet at all for the rest of the night" if you compulsively check your email or Facebook during work hours.

- Write a mantra and stick it on your wall where you can see it

This could be a quote, song lyrics or something else that reminds you of what you want to achieve. You can change the mantra according to your mood and when other things distract you from working on your goal. It's easier to remember what's written in front of your face than something that is in the back of your mind.

The power of writing things down and keeping them visible is huge. Mantras could touch on your work ethic, ethics, morals, and human values. For example:

"*I am so much better than I was yesterday."*

"*Whatever I do will be better than what I did yesterday."*

"*This makes me feel that I'm following my inner guidance or something bigger than myself."*

- Identify your procrastination triggers

Have a list of challenges such as social activity, bad food choices, a stressful environment, physical pain, or illness. Write down what you do when you procrastinate. This will help you to find a pattern in your actions and make it easier to overcome. A mindful approach will be more effective as this will allow you to accept any stress that happens in your life so that you won't overreact or procrastinate.

Maybe you procrastinate when you're at home and you feel like you're wasting time. You get easily distracted by your family, pets, or the TV. At work, you procrastinate when you're feeling stressed or there's too much work that needs to be done. The more stressed out you get the more distracted you get and the more likely it is that frustrating thoughts arises in your mind such as "I'm not good enough", "I'm stupid" and "I can't do this." When you take on too many things at once, this could be one of the reasons why you procrastinate.

Find your triggers and eliminate them. If you're at home, go for a walk outside by yourself or with a friend. If you're feeling stressed at work, try to talk to your boss or co-workers. Exercise can also help reduce stress and give you more energy.

- Create specific deadlines

This will make you feel a sense of urgency and so you'll work faster to meet the deadline. You'll work more on the tasks when you keep track of your progress. For example, I made a to do list in Evernote which slowly fills up as I complete each task, it makes me want to do them all as quickly as possible.

A sense of urgency would make it easier to focus on the task at hand. Instead of worrying about what everyone else thinks of you or whether you're doing something right or wrong, you'll just focus on getting the task done.

Deadlines will also make it easier to walk away from distractions. You might feel like you have wasted time if you're procrastinating but at least you know that your task is on a deadline and that more work needs to be done on it.

Timeboxing is when you set a time limit to your tasks, for example 30 minutes. In Getting Things Done by David Allen, he suggests setting a timer to work on your tasks and then taking time out. I find that timeboxing works well as you can just let go of the task at hand and not worry about it until the time is up. When you set a timer, you're giving yourself permission to stop working and do something else for now. The deadline will help you focus on working faster once the timer is up. You'll feel more accomplished when checking off the task.

Overcoming procrastination is one of those things that can change your life if you allow it to.

When it is okay to procrastinate

At times, it's okay to procrastinate. You might have a very important task or project on hand, or you might be extremely tired, sick or stressed out. Maybe you had a stressful day at work, and you just don't feel like doing anything else. You could put your tasks off until tomorrow (or whenever you feel more motivated) and just relax now. This doesn't mean that you're lazy, it means that there's a pattern in your habits and you want to change those. It is an unconscious pattern, so it takes some time to change it into a more positive one.

You might have taken on too much work and you feel overwhelmed by it. You need to take a break so that you can return with a fresh mind. This can prevent you from getting too stressed out by working at it non-stop. Burnout happens when you feel so overwhelmed by your work that you can't see a way out. You could stop working for a while to let your mind clear. Burnout is one of the biggest reasons why people procrastinate. Maybe take some time off and do something more relaxing such as read a book, go for a walk, or watch TV.

Maybe you need more time to weigh up the decisions. Maybe you want to speak with the person in charge or try to get more information from them before making a decision.

You could leave it until tomorrow or later if it's a big decision like signing up for something new at work or buying an expensive car. When you don't have all the information you need, it's okay to put it off for now. You don't want to make a decision until you have all the information because it might affect other important things in your life, such as investing and paying taxes on it.

You could put it off for a week or two and then reassess at a later date. Procrastination isn't always bad. At times, it's a good thing. Some people struggle with procrastination but still manage to accomplish amazing things. Perhaps you have a lot on your plate right now and need to take a break, take some time to think over some important matters or get more information. Maybe you want to speak with the person in charge or try to get more information from them before making a decision.

It's not okay to just put your tasks off until later. You need to work on it now, ideally when you have time to work on it. If you wait until tomorrow, you'll probably procrastinate every day. It's okay to take a break if you're struggling with something.

CHAPTER 9: BALANCING WORK AND LIFE

Is there a difference between being a workaholic and overworking yourself? Maybe. When you put in an extra hour at the workplace, when you work an extra hour at home and when you work 10 hours a day, when you go the extra mile, are you really being productive? We hate to admit it, but the answer is no. Spending 12+ hours a day working doesn't always equal being productive. In fact, it often means the complete opposite. When put under too much pressure and stress, your body naturally starts to fight back.

Stress is the mind's way of telling the body that something is wrong. Not only does stress cause emotional reactions within yourself but it also has a direct physiological impact on your body. As a result, we often make mistakes when we are tired or stressed out. Exhaustion causes us to forget things and makes us slower at tasks that need precision. In short, our bodies are not meant to be overworked.

Too much work can be a problem because: You're overworking yourself; your productivity will be greatly reduced. You'll feel tired, grumpy, irritable, or sick most of the time. A healthy work life balance means that you have time to relax and rest with your friends or family.

<u>Why's balancing work and personal life important?</u>

- You'll feel happier

More time spent doing the things that matter most to you will result in a much better quality of life. It's easy to get caught up in your obsession with work, neglecting many crucial aspects of your life that make you human. At the end of the day, we all want to be happy and when we put our personal needs first, we're much more likely to achieve our goals. Stressful work environments are bad for your health and are particularly harmful for our physical and mental well-being.

When you spend too much time working on something, it becomes an obligation rather than something you want to do. Think back to when you first started playing football or riding bikes with your friends as a kid. Let's say that you're doing the same thing for a living. Will it still be fun? Maybe. A healthy working relationship with your colleagues will ensure that you're not going against someone else's goals. You'll be much more successful in the long run.

When you're tired and overworked, it's very easy to make mistakes. When this happens, you have to go back and fix these mistakes or think of alternative ways to complete a project that are more efficient. This tires you out even more because this time it's due to stress instead of exhaustion. It also means that you have less time for your family, friends, or social activities in general.

- Our time in this world is finite

"I wish I had spent more hours at the office," said no one ever. When the time for the inevitable comes, when you realize that your body is no longer in prime shape, when the angel of death comes to take you away, you don't want to spend your last days running around the office trying to finish up projects that you barely have time for. You want to relax and enjoy the time you have with your family and friends because when these moments arrive, they won't come back. They're gone forever.

Two professors at the University of Illinois did a study on the biggest regrets people had at their deathbed and the second most popular one was "I wish I hadn't worked so hard." Let that sink in.

For many of us, work is only a means to an end, just like it's supposed to be. It should never be the end goal; it should be a means to an overall greater objective. Working, like everything else in life, is meant to make you happy. If it isn't doing that, you're doing it wrong.

Working hard is not the same as working smart

There's a misconception out there that in order to succeed, you need to go all out until your face turns blue and you collapse due to exhaustion. The problem with this is that just because you're working hard, or long hours doesn't mean you're producing quality work. Sure, if your job requires you to assemble things in a factory, then yes; production does equate work. But what about other professions? If a teacher has 15 extra hours of marking and planning for next term, does that really mean he's been productive? No. It just shows how far behind he is on his workload for the current season. Yes, you're working hard, but are you also working smart?

- Everything in moderation

Party too hard on Sunday and the hangover might prevent you from going to work on Monday. Work too hard for one week and your family might feel neglected for another. You can't go on a binge and expect everything to be perfect every single time. When it comes to having a well-rounded life, there needs to be a balance between our work, personal, and social lives. Many people neglect their personal lives in favor of building up their career because they mistake being productive with being successful. But in reality, they're just so tired, stressed out and burned out that they'd rather sleep or do something else instead of continuing the loop of stress and burnout that has become part of their daily routine.

When you're in your 20s, when you're just starting out, you can manage to get a lot of things done. But when you're in your 30s and are already in your second or third job, it becomes a whole different ballgame. You're no longer starting from scratch, and you're no longer taught how to make efficient use of your time. When we start working, we don't make the best use of our time because it's new to us and as such, we don't know how to spend it wisely.

But over time, if you really want to achieve something bigger and become more successful, you need to learn how to make the most out of the hours that you have on the clock.

A screen-free lunch break

The typical workplace gives a one-hour lunch break. That's all the time you have to yourself to do whatever you want. You can eat, sleep, catch up on Netflix, or a combination of these. How do you spend this time? The way I do it, is by turning off my computer and phone and instead, doing something productive.

- Eat lunch outdoors

Why is eating outdoors so much more interesting than eating inside? I'm not entirely sure, but it's a lot better than having a meal while looking at the screen of your phone. And even if you're taking pictures or videos of your meal, you're still paying attention to the visual stimuli present in front of you instead of the real world right in front of your eyes. Unless you're uploading said pictures or videos to your social media accounts (and why are you doing that while at work?), there's no need to be on your phone while eating lunch.

If there's a nice outdoor restaurant near your office, then by all means, go there. It's a nice change of scenery and since you're not on your phone all the time, you get to actually enjoy your meal.

It doesn't have to be fancy. A simple mom and pop restaurant with a patio is just as nice.

- Take a nap or get some fresh air

Studies have shown that when you're not looking at a computer screen, your brain releases endorphins that make you feel happier and more energetic. When you take lunch and spend it doing something meaningful, it has the same effect on your brain and body. Go for a walk if you can, but if not, try to at least get up for 5 minutes every hour so that your legs don't cramp up from sitting in one position for hours on end.

Another great way to clear the clutter in your head and mind is to go and grab some fresh air outside. Pretend that you're being serenaded by a beautiful song. The fresh air will clear your head and make you feel better overall. I know that it sounds silly, but I've found that it does work, and it helps me quite a bit when I'm having trouble getting work done. It's easy to spend so much of your day on the computer. It's an easy comfort zone for many people. People who are punctual for their job are probably people who appreciate their job but aren't necessarily fanatics about it either. Squeeze in a workout if you can. This may not always be possible, but if you have time at lunch and nothing else to do, then try to squeeze in some exercise. Get up and walk around the block. Try to go on a walk outside while eating your lunch. Take a short run or bike ride before or after work. It doesn't take much time and it can give you lots of energy for the rest of the day and make you feel happier overall.

- Find something mundane, boring, and/or not work related to do during lunch

Call a friend, call your mom, or read a book or magazine. This is a great way to escape from your work day and be able to focus on something completely boring and uninteresting for hours at a time. You know you can read 50 Shades of Gray for hours on end. Everyone can read 50 Shades of Gray for hours on end.

- Take part in office activities

If you're lucky enough to have one, join an office activity group. The more often you get together and spend time doing something together, the more comfortable you'll become talking to strangers and being around other people. You'll also be able to build connections with people who work in the same building as you and just generally make a lot of friends that way. I don't know about your office, but at my workplace, we like to break away from the routine every now and then and do something fun while we're out of the office.

Balancing work and family

You're a hardworking dad/mom who wants to do what's best for your family and your children. You're working long hours. Not only that, but you're often commuting back and forth between work and home. How do you balance all of this and still be able to make time for the family?

This is a tough question to answer because there are so many ways that people find to balance their personal life with a career. But it's doable.

- Put your spouse, kids, and extended family on the calendar

In the same way that you plan for meetings, schedule tasks based on their deadlines, and plan for days off, you need to also plan for your family time. This doesn't necessarily mean that you schedule Sundays for family time (although if you have the opportunity, why not?), but make sure that you're making time for your family and on the calendar so that it's dedicated time in your mind. If your day off is during the weekend and you have to work then, plan for it by getting out of the office early on Friday. It means more time for your family, but it also means that you're working a shorter day. It's all about balance, right?

If you're lucky enough to be able to take advantage of great parental leave policies, take them. Don't feel bad if you want (or need) to spend more time with your family. Ask for help from loved ones or ask your colleagues if they can cover for you while you go and spend time with your family. You won't be doing anyone a favor if you're not happy with work/life balance because then everyone around you will be affected negatively by it.

- Don't travel as much

Again, this is easier said than done since many jobs require travel or involve a lot of frequent travel. But if you can avoid business trips and instead, take vacations with the family instead of being away all week at a conference in another city, then go ahead and do it. Every time you're travelling, you're away from your family and they're unhappy because they don't get to see you. Plus, you're spending money on airfare and hotel rooms, which means less money for the family to do fun things together. If a business trip is an absolute necessity or if it's unavoidable, then take it. Learn to say no if a trip isn't absolutely necessary for your job or if there's another way of doing the same thing.

If you have the option of working from home relatively often, do it. Your family will benefit from your presence, and you'll be able to spend more time with them. You can make the argument that you're not doing as good of a job or that you're working less efficiently, but remember, your family will be the ones who suffer most.

- Be passionate about family too

I bet that you're a hard worker. You're passionate about your job and you do everything in your power to make ends meet, meet deadlines and to ensure that your clients and bosses are satisfied. Show the same enthusiasm about your family time and about spending time with the people you love. Don't let work come first in your mind at all times. Commit to making it work and to making your family happy.

That's easier said than done because like I said earlier, once you get into the habit of doing a lot of work, it's hard to stop. But sometimes you just have to step back, realize that you're working too much, and that the quality of your work can sometimes be better if you spend more time focusing on it than if you try to squeeze in a bunch of extra hours here and there. I know that this is easier said than done...but just try it.

Make your family a priority too. They're the people you love, and they deserve your time and attention.

- Laugh

Do silly stuff with your children. When you get home from work, play card games, see who can hold their breadth the longest, wash the car together, tell jokes, play hide and seek...whatever you do, do it with a sense of fun. Don't take yourself too seriously. Had a long day at work? Don't bring it home with you. Leave it at work and be the fun dad or mom when you're with the family. Be silly and make a joke about something silly that happened to you throughout the day. It's just a way to let go of stress, so take part in it.

Spend time with your wife or husband discussing how things are going at work. Ask them what they thought of their day and how they think things went as well as what they expect tomorrow will look like. Also, talk about your troubles at work together and don't be afraid to share your fears, anxieties, or concerns about work (or family) with the person closest to you – your partner/spouse/etc... Take it easy.

- Hire a bedsitter

You need to spend time with your wife too. Get a trustworthy babysitter and go out on a special date with your wife. Or just have a night of the two of you while the kids are asleep; you can watch TV, have some wine, do whatever you want to do. At the end of the day, work isn't all that matters. Your wife is your partner and she's been with you through everything so it's important to spend time together. Remember, your boss won't be the one who'll suffer from all of these changes. Your family will be the ones who suffer.

Stress management

There are bills to be paid, a mortgage to be serviced, kids to feed...life isn't all sunshine and roses. But it doesn't have to be that way. If you can learn to handle stress in the most productive and efficient manner possible, then it will save a lot of time and money for you because you'll spend less time working and more time doing things that are important to you.

There are two types of stress:

1) Micro/minute-to-minute stress: as the name suggests, this type of stress is small incidents where there's a little bit of tension or pressure coming from outside sources (boss, colleagues, etc.) When these situations occur, your body responds by releasing stress hormones.

2) Macro/hourly-to-hourly stress: this type of stress is more common and often more severe. It's a general feeling of pressure and tension that builds up throughout the day or week and can be relieved only after long periods of time have passed. The end result? You feel like you're stressed out of your mind because there's no way you can get things done.

When it comes to handling these types of stress, there are actually some great ways to do it. Meditation, taking time to yourself, exercise and relaxation are all great stress relievers.

There are many ways to meditate. Some people like to observe their breath, some like to observe the patterns that appear on the walls and some like to listen to music. No matter which way you do it, the end result is always positive. The idea behind meditation is that by just sitting down and doing nothing, your mind slowly becomes more relaxed, and your worries become less significant. After a few minutes (or hours for more advanced practitioners), you'll feel more at ease about life and work in general. You can do it on a daily basis or weekly basis.

Listen to a guided meditation and take the full advantage of its benefits by using it to reduce stress and anxiety.

Working out releases endorphins, which are the body's own natural mood boosters. They help you feel calmer and happier. So even if you don't feel like it, remember to get yourself some exercise – even just moving around at home while doing things that you normally do every day will help relieve stress.

It doesn't have to be a rigorous workout. You don't need to run 10 kilometers a day. You can just do a half hour of pushups at the end of a workday and you'll feel like you've accomplished something.

Have a hobby. You don't have to have a special hobby that has to be difficult like playing the piano. You can just learn something new, do a few things at once and the result is that your stress level drops dramatically. It doesn't even have to be something directly related to work (if you can do what you do at work on top of it) but it should be something that you enjoy doing.

Learning to say no

At times when we have too much work on our plates, our bosses and our clients expect more from us than we can give. When these situations arise there's always a choice to say "no." But sometimes, when you're worried about losing your job or being seen as less than an important member of the team, it can be difficult to say no. When you're THAT team player who always goes above and beyond, it's hard to face people who come in and say, "we only hire the best" and then look at you as if you're not important enough to be hired. So, smile, nod and keep saying "no" as often as possible. Be clear with your boss what exactly you can do to help the company. Then when someone asks you for your opinion or for help with a project, assist them without being asked for it. It might not seem like much, but it will take time off their hands of things they have to do and make them more likely to allow you some liberty with your time too!

When you don't say no to others, when you pick up more tasks than you should be doing, you become extremely stressed out. It's like you're trapped in a never-ending cycle of being pressured by others to help them with their work, your work piling up and more work being assigned to you. But if you learn to say no, then things become simpler for everyone. You'll have less stress because you aren't doing more than what is expected of you, others will have less problems because they aren't working under the pressure of an overzealous person who has taken on too many tasks and the management will be able to manage the amount of work that goes out to each person individually without having some people being overworked while others are overly relaxed or bored. Here's how you could say no at the workplace without offending your colleagues (and getting fired):

- Be clear when you are saying no.

Don't just lie and say "no, I'm not busy." Be specific: "no, I can't this weekend." "I will complete this task on a different date. Remember, you're striving for a healthy work life balance where you can enjoy as much time with your family and friends as you can. So, we need you to always keep that in mind. Remember that saying "no" is almost never personal. It's the lack of time, it's the fact that you have so much on your plate that you don't have time to be a teenager in a part-time job at your local mall. Be courteous and explain yourself as soon as possible.

Let your teammates, workers, bosses, coworkers, etc. know that you're a reliable and important part of the team but you won't be able to come in over the weekend or to a "meet and greet" at the office and so on.

Of course, you need to assess the request before you reject it. If you have the time and the skill, for example, do you really want to say no to that request for help? If the task is something that does not require much of your time, then by all means step up and volunteer. You'll be doing a good deed that can sometimes be overlooked in corporate culture: being a team player. In fact, it's critical in this phase of your life where you're still building your professional resume and networking.

However, when the task requires a huge time commitment or you don't have the expertise to complete it, it's better not to accept the task. Being a people pleaser isn't always the best way to be, and for you, being a people pleaser would take time away from your developmental resume. Now is not the time to be sucking up to your boss or doing favors for others so they can feel important. You will never know how this request will later benefit you in your career and job search.

- Be courteous and polite

Remember, saying no is a basic skill of life. It's not necessarily a bad thing. If you can always try to explain why you are not able to do something, then you will be able to receive fewer and fewer requests in the future that you have to reject. For example, when someone starts pressuring you for a favor, be courteous and concise about it. Saying "no" needs two parties working together – one who says it, and one who hears it – so as much as possible, explain why or how you cannot assist them and thank them for their time.

If possible, give alternatives or refer them to someone else who can help out. For example, if your boss asks for something you cannot do, you can say "I'm sorry, but I am too busy right now. Maybe Jane could take over the project." If a co-worker asks you to help but you already have too much on your plate to do it, suggest that they approach another coworker or a member of management instead.

Switching off from work

How can we switch from 'working mode' to 'relaxing mode' at the end of the day? We shouldn't be bringing homework related stresses and worries. But we all do for a variety of reasons. At times we're pressured by our boss, or we feel like we need to keep up with the group or we are simply working on a tight project where the deadline is imminent. But this is a recipe for disaster.

Make sure you take some time out of your day to relax and unwind. The amount of stress we feel at the workplace can be debilitating if not taken care of immediately. If you are not careful, it will manifest itself in bad ways: stress headaches, hair thinning, and most importantly you'll feel unhappy with your life. All it takes is a few minutes every day to ease your mind and get you feeling refreshed and ready for the next day at work.

Coming home from work and taking care of things before you relax is important but it will not make the situation any better if you have to do so by worrying about work. You need to take that time out of your life. You should be spending that time with your friends, family, loved ones and yourself (don't forget, love yourself first!). Work shouldn't follow you home and invade your personal space after a 9 to 5 job because it shouldn't affect your quality of life any way unless it's absolutely necessary.

You need to make a point of acknowledging the end of your working day and the changing over into 'relaxing mode'.

- Start by acknowledging your limits

Accept that you're not an Udarnik who's working like crazy all the time. Your boss is probably not going to scream or insult you if you bring your work home with you or say anything at all. You will likely find that your colleagues don't mind either and even may encourage you to do so. If you're afraid that this is going to result in a downer of a day and an irritable person bringing homework, accept the fact that you cannot be an Udarnik 24/7 and then remind yourself that it's okay not to have an amazing day every single time, but it's a must to set realistic standards for yourself.

You should have realistic standards for yourself in work and life. Know how much work you can accomplish on a given day, know when it's okay to go home, and know what to do with all that free time that you're going to have. If you're not feeling enthusiastic about the end of your day at work, start that evening by acknowledging that you're feeling down before you head out the door.

Then, create an exit list. That's exactly like it sounds - a list of tasks that you'll do and after that, you're calling it a day. It might be washing the dishes, folding laundry, or cleaning up clutter. After you're done with these work-related tasks, you won't feel so stressed, and you'll be able to enjoy your day.

CHAPTER 10: DECLUTTERING

We're naturally hoarders. Maybe we evolved to collect food and other provisions for lean times. In medieval times when the weather was unpredictable, "hoarding" meant stocking up on food and other supplies. In the contemporary world where food abounds, we've adapted our hoarding tendencies to all sorts of stuff — from CDs and DVDs to toys, books, clothes and more.

The amount of stuff in our lives is staggering. In 2009, Americans spent an estimated $87 billion on entertainment (such as music and movies) alone. The tab for books is even higher at $84 billion. Meanwhile the average American family owns more than $87,000 worth of stuff.

That's a lot of stuff. And most people can't seem to keep it organized or out of the landfill — despite numerous organizational plans, primers and books written on the subject.

We hold onto stuff for the sentimental value — like a tattered, old album cover or ticket stub. But we should put more effort into preventing clutter from taking hold of our lives in the first place. We can't expect new, shiny stuff to replace what we already own. That's where a ruthless approach comes in handy.

Having too much stuff and not knowing what to do with it is like having the flu — it's no fun at all.

The organized person keeps only needed items on hand so that he or she can live comfortably and efficiently without chasing after what he or she needs from his or her stuff.

And when you're unorganized, not only do you suffer from the stress of searching for misplaced items, but your stuff has a tendency to multiply out of control.

Even if you don't realize it, your stuff is an energy drain that saps your energy and stresses you out. It's probably why clutterbugs on average have less energy, more health problems and are unhappier than their organized counterparts.

Decluttering can bring clarity to even the messiest home or office — making it easier to tackle any problems lurking in the background.

What's more, minimalism can bring balance to an otherwise out-of-control life. It is a way to restore order to a hectic schedule while clearing the mental space you need in order to focus on the things that matter most.

We'll look at how you can minimize your stuff and maximize your life.

That floppy disk or old cassette tape that you can't bear to throw away or give away? Is that heavy volume of books in the corner collecting dust? And is that stack of papers cluttering your desk? Anything you own may fall under the title of clutter. It's not a lot of stuff. It's all the stuff.

We make room for some stuff, and we put others in closets, but we fill our houses and offices with too many possessions. There's just too much stuff. We've gotten used to owning a lot, but we forget what it's like to live with very little.

There's no joy in hoarding unless we're diligent about organizing our stuff and clearing the clutter. That's why you need to declutter — if for no other reason than for your sake. It's not just good for your home and office, it's good for your health, too.

Forgetting an item at the grocery store doesn't mean we need to keep it in our refrigerator forever. This is why we have expiration dates on food. We make room for new stuff by making room for old stuff to go away. It's like spring cleaning: you get rid of the old to make room for the new. In fact, spring cleaning and decluttering are pretty much the same thing — only you clean out closets rather than windowsills and mow the lawn rather than wash your car.

What's clutter?

It's not just physical items that fill up our space. Worry, fear, anxiety, and paranoia are mental clutter. They're just as bad for your health as physical clutter:

Mental clutter diminishes freedom and effectiveness like physical clutter does. If a cluttered desk makes you late, a cluttered mind makes you inefficient. If a cluttered desk raises your stress level, a cluttered mind reduces your creativity. Clutter creates distance between the intender and the intention.

What physical clutter does to our body

You can't sit still and focus on the clutter around you. It's like your body feels uncomfortable when there's too much stuff and it feels uncomfortable when there's too little stuff.

Like an overflowing closet, a cluttered office or room is hard to organize and clean. You've got to sift through everything, find what you need, put the rest away and then clean up the mess.

A cluttered mind is one that's filled with doubts and worries in need of sorting. This can trigger stress, which is physically taxing on your body.

It affects our mental well-being. Cortisol is a hormone released by your adrenal glands that increases your heart rate, blood pressure, sugar, and fat levels — which is why a stressful event can make you hungry. What's more, cortisol seems to reduce the activity of the prefrontal cortex — which controls decision-making and self-awareness. When our living space is cluttered, our mind can't rest. The stress of a cluttered mind can make you less productive, decrease your memory and lower your self-esteem.

What physical clutter does to our mind

Our minds are cluttered with things we need to remember, figures we need to compute, problems we need to solve — and the clutter takes over our thoughts. What's worse is that it interferes with creative thinking, which is why unorganized offices are often uninspired places.

If we can't get our minds to a clear state of thought, we can't get our hands to a clear state of action. We need creative thinking and decision-making, but all too often these are hampered by clutter. Clutter in the mind means stress, tension, and poor decision-making. And that makes us less productive.

What it does to our money

You can spend a lot of money on storage alone and even more on moving it around. And that doesn't even get into the money you spend on outfitting your house or office.

Is it worth it? Does it really cost that much to buy things, to move them in, to organize and clean them?

How much does your stuff cost? If you have too much stuff, take a look at these costs:

The value of your time— since you have to find what you're looking for, put away what's out of place and clean up what's messy. That is time that could have been better spent doing something else — like watching TV or reading the paper. And don't forget the time you spent buying the stuff.

Storage space — where you have to pay for shelves and cupboards and filing cabinets to keep your stuff. This is no small expense if you live in a large city like New York or Los Angeles. Transportation costs — having to move it from one place to the other adds time, effort, and money since you have to pay people, get a truck and fill it up.

Maintenance costs (like taxes, insurance, and warranties) — these can add up when something breaks or wears out, which means paying someone else to fix them or spending more money on new things.

The 4 types of Mental clutter

Worry, negative self-talk, anxiety, and fear are forms of mental clutter. It's often a state of mind that starts when you have too many things in too little space. But it doesn't have to stay there.

Mental clutter is a form of worry that robs our minds of clarity and focus. It's something we feel inside, rather than something someone can point out to us in the physical world, like piles of dirty dishes on the counter or moldy rice on the floor. It's more than just a list of concerns; it sabotages our ability to think clearly and make good decisions.

Negative self-talk

Self-talk is what we tell ourselves all day long: "I'm going to fail," "I'm not smart enough," "This is too hard" — and so on. It's a form of internal chatter that doesn't need to be said out loud, but to us it might as well be. It's the voice inside that tells us we're not good enough, smart enough or ready for what lies ahead. Self-limiting beliefs are self-talk that holds us back from being who we could be.

We sabotage ourselves in so many ways — we don't apply for that job because we think we're not qualified, or we don't finish the big project or research paper because it seems beyond our abilities. We'll never really know what's beyond our abilities — and what's not — if we don't give it a shot.

It's not just negative self-talk, it can be fear and worry as well. Fear is worry about the future. It can be about one particular thing or all things in general — but whatever it is, fear is always mental clutter. Fear is what we feel inside when stress, pressure or uncertainty is on the rise. It's a feeling of uneasiness about the future or, in some cases, the present or past. Fear can be about our health, finances, family, or friends. It can even arise just to keep us on our toes, so we don't get too comfortable with where we are in life. Fear keeps us alert and alive — unless it becomes an obsession that paralyzes us and makes living a nightmare rather than a dream.

We don't have to be driven by fear or self-doubt. We can learn to feel calm, peaceful, and relaxed. We can learn to quiet our minds, even at the times we feel under pressure and stress. And we can learn from our fears, so they no longer have power over us.

The way that we mentally organize ourselves also affects how physical clutter affects us. If you have a cluttered mind, you'll have a more difficult time getting organized in the physical world.

Clutter is a state of mind. It's something we don't see and can't touch — but it still affects us. It affects our bodies, our health, our productivity and, in some cases, our very lives.

Mental saturation is the feeling we experience when there's just too much to think about. Our brains simply can't process the information coming at them fast enough — thus we feel mentally overloaded.

Getting rid of mental clutter

So how do we get rid of mental clutter? Easy — just like physical clutter.

Choose what to keep and what to toss. If we can't choose, then it doesn't belong in our lives anyway. Most of the time it's stuff that isn't serving us or things that have outlived their purpose or have no purpose at all — like receipts, old newspapers, magazines, and emails you don't need to save for any reason. Are you worried about it or thinking about it? If not, then it doesn't need to be in your life. Keep what's important because clutter is anything we don't need or want in our lives. If you're not sure about what to keep and what to toss, ask yourself if you would lose something if you lost a particular item. If the answer is "yes" — keep it where you can find it!

The key to getting rid of mental clutter is the same as getting rid of physical clutter:

Rule out fear and worry by dealing with things that make us nervous. Deal with your fears before they deal with you! Never ignore them because they'll just continue to grow until they're eating up all of your time and energy.

- Be mindful

This is where you observe what's going on without judging it. You're not thinking about how you "should" be feeling, or what you "should" be doing next — you just notice what's going on inside and outside of yourself. When your mind starts to bother you with thoughts about the past or future, bring it back to the here and now. Mindfulness is the practice of living in the now.

Don't beat yourself up for the past. It's over, you can't change it and you can't live in it anyway so there is no point beating yourself up over decisions made years ago. Allow yourself to be proud of what you did then, but don't let it control your present or future. You're not defined by the past — even if were horrible events brought on by negative self-talk, we still have a choice to make about how we act today from that point forward. We have choices every day to put what happened in the past behind us — or not — and live a good life accordingly.

- Chop down your to do list

You don't need to be doing everything all the time. As I said before, it's impossible for us to do everything in this world — that would be insane — so we need to learn to prioritize and know what's important. Think of your to do list as a list of priorities; what you need to do and what can wait. Sometimes we don't need an excuse for procrastinating, sometimes we simply have too many choices and should prioritize accordingly. In case you haven't noticed yet, that's what the To Do list is for!

Chop down everything on your to do list. If you have a task that you're putting off for a long time, ask yourself if you really need to do it. Don't beat yourself up over an incomplete project or a missed deadline — we all miss things because we have deadlines and life happens, we're human and so is paperwork. Simply make another plan, let it go and move on with the rest of your day.

- Be gentle with yourself

There will always be those times when mental clutter becomes too much for us to handle. It's OK to let yourself off the hook and simply let it go. We'll all do that sometimes if we need to — it's all part of being a human. Be patient. This is the hardest thing for us to learn in life, we want things NOW! We're impatient, we want everything yesterday so we can play, relax, and concentrate on more important things tomorrow — like paying bills or completing our projects.

You can't change the past, nor can you predict the future. Nobody is perfect and nobody will do everything right all the time. Life happens and no matter how hard we try or how much we "should" do, sometimes we just don't have time to be perfect. Be kind to yourself and give yourself credit when you're doing good. Find a balance between wanting things too much (like perfection) and wanting them too little (missing deadlines).

The minimalist game

Physical clutter is easy to spot — it's right there in front of us. Mental clutter, however, is not always so clear. We can't see it because we're inside of our heads, experiencing thoughts and feelings, but we can still feel it — nonetheless.

The key is being aware. Like physical clutter, mental clutter can be a hindrance to our productivity and time management skills. It's something we need to be able to recognize when we're feeling stressed out or overwhelmed by too many mundane tasks every day.

Physical clutter is easier to deal with though. Organizing experts recommend keeping your surroundings — especially the items we use every day — in an orderly and clean manner to minimize clutter and maximize productivity.

- Don't dump small things on tables

Your wallet, phone, car keys, and other items shouldn't be placed haphazardly on your desk or in a pile on the floor. Keep them in their own containers and keep them organized to make finding what you're looking for easier. Instead have designated 'catch all' trays where miscellaneous items go. Under bench storage may be another option.

Everything has a place, especially your clutter that can easily be misplaced or stowed away when you aren't looking at it. Consider hanging baskets with removable bins or baskets near your desk to collect unwanted items that you'll get rid of after their use is done.

Hooks and shelves are also a great way to stay organized and keep clutter off your desk. Hooks are perfect for hanging your keys, baskets, bags, and anything else without utilizing valuable desk space. Shelves can hold printers, large sized folders, books, and binders amongst other things.

- Find a place for everything

Declutter by in one location and stow away in another location right where it belongs before it piles up on the tabletop or overflowing from drawers/cabinets etc. Shoes should be on the rack, items like keys and pens, in a container. Coats and handbags should be hung up to avoid the 'cluttered look'.

The living room can be a great place for various items. The family room or den, especially in an organized home, may be an ideal spot for jewelry, scarves, and other accessories. Storage trays and baskets can keep keys, cords and loose threads neatly stored away when not in use. Just provide a place to put things away!

Your desk is where you spend most of your time at work and at home so it should be where you keep your non-work related items as well. Keep all your documents close together, in one spot (don't have to have it on the front page of each document). Your organizational system should have pockets all over it; use them to store important papers or valuables such as photographs & gifts etc.

- Be mindful about incoming documents

Be careful about what you allow into your space because before you know it, it turns into clutter. Have a folder or bin set aside for bills to go straight from the mailbox when they arrive and save anything else for later. If you need to make room on your desk, then have an inbox or something else designated that is used only for incoming mail and not as storage space or somewhere to dump things.

Receipts and invoices are easy to misplace, or not see until it's too late. You may only need certain documents for a short period of time and filing everything away can be unneeded. If you want to hang onto them anyway, then invest in some colorful hanging folders that are different from your usual ones, so they stand out and you know not to toss the receipts into a pile on your desk.

Service providers usually offer electronic copies of their invoices — have them sent directly since there is no need to print off an excess of copies that will only end up in the waste bin.

Papers get misplaced when they are thrown in with other documents, have them in a designated spot where they can be easily found. Keep a bin/tray close by for all the papers you will need on hand to read through later. It's best to keep your reading material close at hand so you don't have to run around looking for it when you want it.

- Choose a filing system that works for you

If there are too many cabinets, drawers, and other storage containers, then file things away efficiently so that things are not lost or difficult to find. Have one box designated only for credit card receipts, another for bank statements, another for income tax returns etc.

- Discard unused items

It's important to comb through every last nook and cranny of your home to properly discard or donate anything that's unused or no longer needed. Be sure to keep an eye on items you buy because they often end up going unused or put away until the next time you need them. Space and time are valuable, so keep it clean, simple and clutter-free.

Do you really need to have so many lamps? How about extra chargers for your phone, tablet, or other devices? What about all those extra cables that you may have lying around? Identify what your priorities really are and use that to guide you in the decisions you make about items.

When you feel overwhelmed by the number of items in your life, get rid of what you don't need. It's important to set up rules and routines for yourself so that items aren't just tossed aside or put off until later. Have a designated place for everything you own and be sure to get rid of anything that's no longer needed or wanted.

- Change your view of clutter

Your home isn't a storage unit. It's your living space where you live, work, and relax in. Let go of stuff you don't need and let your home be a place that's pleasing to look at, conducive to work and relaxation, and makes you feel good. The key is to surround yourself with things that are useful, loved, beautiful and make your life easier. Use this guide to clear away clutter once and for all!

Duplicate the organization systems you already have in place such as those in your office or living room into the bedroom. Having an organized bedroom will help you feel more rested during the day.

Keep the floor clear and organized. Lay out your clothes for the day on your bed or hang them on a rack. You won't find lost items that way. If you really need to store them, purchase containers with small drawers to keep things sorted and presentable.

Organize your night table by placing all your items in containers in order of use right near where you sleep. Use baskets or drawers to hold books, magazines, stationery etc. Place all remotes, clocks etc. in one place so they are not scattered around the room. Use hooks and shelves to keep shoes and bags off the floor and out of sight when not in use.

- There's joy in giving

Don't just throw things away because you feel like they no longer have any use. If you pay attention to what you own, then you'll be able to realize exactly how much space is needed for all the items and how they are used in your life. If a certain object isn't as useful anymore, donate it or sell it to make room for something that might be better suited for your needs.

Generosity is giving freely of oneself and your possessions. Know the value of what you own and the use that it serves in terms of daily activities. Identify those items that can be donated to someone else so that they can benefit from it as well. Whatever you don't need anymore, then pass on to another person or family in need without any strings attached; they will be glad to have something useful as opposed to something sitting around taking up space.

- Contain your clutter

Buy decent looking clutter baskets. This is where all your miscellaneous items should be put, and they should be designed to look pretty. They will also keep things organized and visible. Be creative with the design, but a level shelf or basket with ample space is a must if you are to be able to store everything. You can make them match your other decorative items in your room if that appeals to you.

You can paint or cover the baskets or get some of those plastic storage containers like the ones in restaurants that come in different shapes and sizes and keep your things in them. Use smaller baskets for jewelry, makeup, clothes etc.

If you don't want to clutter up the house with baskets, then use a room divider or bookshelf. This is where you place all your things, so they are easy to find and in an organized fashion.

- Put everything away every day

Allocate a designated drawer or cabinet for each type of item that doesn't have its own designated spot such as skincare items, accessories etc. Otherwise, household items can get mixed up and become virtually impossible to keep track of.

Don't leave things in the same spot for days on end. If you do, no one will know that it's there and they'll continue to inadvertently reach into that space without thinking and possibly confuse what they actually should be doing.

Return items to their rightful spot or container when you're finished using them. This ensures that everything is as it should be and also makes you more aware of what's missing when you have to go looking for it later.

Find out what you really need instead of just stuffing things in drawers without much thought. If there are extra items that can no longer be used or are duplicates of what's there, then discard them or put them up for sale on a classified site.

If the space in your drawers is limited and you find yourself running out of room, then use dividers to keep things organized such as scarves, wallets, jewelry etc.

- Multipurpose kitchen appliances are space saving

Instead of getting two different devices to perform the same function, opt for a multipurpose appliance instead. For instance, a toaster oven can be used as an air fryer and a dehydrator while a rice cooker can make noodles, rice, soups etc. It's unnecessary to have multiple appliances around if you have one that will do the job of two or more.

- Go digital

There are so many applications on your phone that you no longer have to fill up spaces with books. You can have hundreds of books stored in your phone and read them just like you would in an actual book. This saves space for other items such as stationery or small baskets for cosmetics etc.

Newspapers and magazines can be downloaded from the internet and put on your tablet. This saves room in your home. You no longer have to keep so much collected material around as a reference for all kinds of things such as fashion trends, news updates, sports scores, recipes etc.

When we're emotionally attached to stuff

Emotional clutter is a lot different from the physical kind. Some people love collecting things because they can't let go of them, even if they're no longer useful. Others are just trying to fill their homes up with things that they think that they need or want whether it's realistic or not. It might be easier to let go of this kind of clutter rather than the physical kind as it doesn't take up as much room in your home. If you have sentimental items such as photos, save them digitally and store them in a safe place rather than leave them lying around on tables or counters.

If you love to collect things like coins, stamps, or watches, then keep them in an accessible place such as a jar on your kitchen counter. You can also get a small coin sorter if you want to sort through your collection regularly.

Is it practical or is it just beautiful? Don't just keep things in your home just because they're beautiful or because you couldn't part with them. Be realistic and think of the actual functionality they can provide to your daily activities.

You need to discover how much value each and every item that you own can bring you, whether it's a valuable antique, an heirloom passed down from generations or a favorite piece of jewelry. Once you've realized the worth, then it's easy to make decisions regarding when to sell and what to keep. If there's something that doesn't bring any amount of value in your life, then don't hold on to it no matter how much sentimental value it might have.

CHAPTER 11: DITCH THE DISTRACTIONS

How many times do you check your phone every day? How many times do you swipe right on Tinder or message your ex? How many times do you browse Instagram or scroll through the newsfeed at night We are constantly bombarded with activities that interfere with our daily tasks. The distractions can get on top of us and be a nuisance to our performance if we don't have a plan of action. Too many distractions make it harder for us to reach our goals and we end up procrastinating more than ever before. When you're distracted, you're no longer present in the moment, and this results in your energy output being variable which ultimately affects your performance negatively.

Social media is designed to be addictive. The number of 'likes' you get on each picture, the number of comments on your posts, and the number of likes you get on your tweets is something that plays on our mind. Each 'like' we get or comment someone makes gives us a sense of achievement. Some people even go so far as to feel empty if they manage to post something without getting much reaction from people around them.

You might not think that social media is a huge distraction in your life, but it is. It's very easy for you to overlook all the times that you're spending hours in front of your laptop or phone every day just scrolling through pages and pages of updates from all over the world, putting yourself into unnecessary stress trying to compete with people who are more successful than what you perceive yourself to be.

It's like we're seeking approval from people we don't know. Some people want to seem busy while others want to appear more cultured or hip by posting the most popular videos on social media. It's possible that this has become a habit that we can't seem to break. We need approval from these strangers and sometimes we try so hard to get it that it consumes our attention span by making us lose sight of what's important. During the time you spend in front of your device, you're not interacting with your loved ones or working on your goals. You could be in the same room as someone else but still be overthinking of what you're going to post on your next Instagram story instead of paying attention to them when they speak.

Social media is the biggest distraction we're having in this age, but it isn't the only one. There are a hundred other things seeking your attention. When you're watching tv, the news keeps flashing headlines. When you're at a party, people keep trying to hook you up with other people or get your attention for something else. When you're out shopping, billboards promote new products and make you wish that you can have them. When you're in the car, radio stations play commercial jingles every 10 minutes or so. These are just some examples of how we are constantly bombarded by distractions from all directions and it's a lot to handle especially when our minds aren't strong enough to go through it on their own without breaking apart.

How do we overcome this?

We should start by identifying the biggest distractor in our lives first. This can be different for everyone, but we need to identify it first before taking action. If you're being distracted by social media, then stop using it and see how long you can go without logging on to Facebook or Instagram. If it's television, try to lower the volume and limit your time watching shows instead of just zoning out while watching an entire season in 1 sitting.

When you feel like you're being distracted, instead of going into a trance like a hypnotized person would do, try doing something productive instead such as reading a book or working on your goals.

Distractions can camouflage themselves as important tasks. When we do things that are of high priority, we get a sense of accomplishment from the process and outsource most of our tasks to others. Instead of working on our goals, we would rather have someone else do it for us. We're not dealing with stress but merely delegating tasks to others which makes us feel good about ourselves but at the same time very lazy in terms of actually doing anything.

Everything that you need to be focusing on whether it's making a meal for your loved ones or making the necessary changes in your life is something that should be done by yourself because only you know what needs to be done.

The difference between important and urgent tasks

When you're deciding what task is important and which one is urgent, there's a difference. Important tasks are those that require you to work on them over and over again like building a good body, staying disciplined or working towards your goals but the urgency of these tasks are not dependent on you. You can forsake these to attend to urgent tasks that need immediate attention. At the workplace for example, an important task would be handing out reports to your colleagues, but a priority task would be dealing with a client who keeps calling you to discuss business matters. An important task would be fitting your workout schedule into your daily life while a priority task would be attending a work event that requires you to look presentable.

Identifying your distractions

Before you eliminate your distractions, you need to identify them first. An example of a distraction could be watching reruns of your favorite TV show every night after your shift is over and not doing anything else as well. This can be a source of comfort since you've done your job and can relax in your own home, but that comfort only comes at the price of forgetting about all the other things that you should be taking care of in order to reach your goals or maintaining some balance in life.

This exercise is used to identify distractions that are causing you anxiety and stress. This will also help you see how much time you're spending on these thoughts and what activities you can do to prevent yourself from being distracted by them.

1. Get a piece of paper and a pen or your phone if that's easier for you to use.

2. Start writing out all the things that are bothering you in your life in the form of questions or answers like this: What is bothering me right now? Why am I bothered by this? What do I want to do about it? What do I think will happen if I don't take care of it?

3. Think of the last time when you were working on a serious task but couldn't seem to finish it. This can be anything, but it should be something that requires a lot of concentration and effort on your part.

4. What distractions did you encounter?

5. What was the most distracting thing that prevented you from finishing your task and how did you handle it? How long did it take to end this distraction (if it didn't, what caused it to continue)?

6. This is important, do any of these distractions become a problem for you when they are not taken care of? If so, what can

be done to prevent this situation from happening in the first place?

7. What tasks do you still have pending that you've failed to complete on time or at all because of distractions? If these are bills or work tasks, then make a plan to finish them on time or at all.

This exercise will help you recognize your weaknesses and also show you how to deal with it by not giving into distractions. Learn to say no to the things that are causing you stress and anxiety or even take away your attention from these matters so you can get things done. It's better to do one task at a time than going in half-assed and achieving nothing at the end of the day.

Eliminating Digital distractions

These are the most common distractions in our lives right now that affects us mentally and physically. The constant bombardment of people on social networks and the noise surrounding us makes it hard to focus on the important tasks in life.

For most of you reading this, your life would be a lot more productive if you were able to eliminate these from your life. The less you care about what other people think, say, or do, the more time you will have for yourself because your energy won't be drained by doing so many other things at once. You will also feel better about yourself for not listening to toxic people who are only trying to put themselves up as an authority by tearing others down just to make themselves feel better about themselves.

Social media isn't just bad because it distracts us when we're working towards our goals. We tend to compare ourselves to other people on these sites and the more we do so, the more anxious we become about whether or not we measure up to what others are doing. This builds anxiety because you're constantly thinking about how good or bad you've done compared to everyone else. In this case, you're not doing your own thing that requires focus and concentration but instead being distracted by what people are doing online.

How do we get rid of these distractions?

- Consider deleting your social media accounts

The first step is to delete all of your social media accounts. Yes, you will be missing out on a lot of things, and it will take some time to re-adapt, but the more you do it, the easier it gets and the better you feel about yourself. Some of us are in careers such as sales where we cannot do this because being on Facebook or Twitter for example can be a great way to generate business for ourselves. If you're in a career that does not rely on social media, then you have a lot more freedom to choose what you'll do with your time.

Delete that game that you've been mindlessly playing for hours. Delete that song on your phone that has been giving you the creeps. Delete that text from a friend who is feeling sorry for themselves because they didn't get what they really wanted in their life.

Turn off these distractions. Whenever you're having lunch with your family, don't use your phone while they are eating with you. It will disrupt their time and rhythms which will make them feel uncomfortable and that's not something that you want to do to them. Instead, just turn off your phone and enjoy spending time with them without anything distracting you from the real world outside of Facebook, YouTube, and Instagram.

- Disable those push notifications

Push notifications are a great way to let you know about things that you care about. You will always see them coming from companies and institutions, but if you're engaging with these distractions, then it's not worth the time. Whenever something comes up that interests you, check it out right away. Block all the notifications that may pop up on your phone until such time when you'll be able to attend to them.

Most phones have a "do not disturb" mode where you can control the notifications. This is also a great way to minimize distractions because you will no longer be subjected to every single notification that comes to your phone.

- Plug of

Are you addicted to the internet? A while ago, I was in a conversation with my colleague, and it was about how we should pursue more in life. We talked about what our goals are and how we can achieve them. It's a good thing to know what you're planning to do in life so that you can be more productive with the time that you have. One of my main goals is learning how to be productive by doing the right things at the right time. I've asked myself why I keep procrastinating on a lot of tasks and it's because I tend to seek distractions all the time.

The internet can be addictive. All those funny cat videos and funny vines that people post on Facebook can be a big distraction if you're not careful. I check the internet when I go to the bathroom in my office, and I always tell myself that I won't get distracted by it because there are other things to do like washing my hands or brushing my teeth. But somehow, I will end up checking out posts on Reddit and get into a conversation with some people about things that have nothing to do with work. After that, I'll ask myself why I feel like wasting time instead of getting stuff done.

- Have a deep focus playlist

This won't work for everyone. Are you most productive when you're listening to music, or do you prefer a quiet, noise-free workplace? If you're like most people, then you like listening to music when you're working on something. Having a deep focus playlist is also a way for you to get into the zone and keep yourself going. I've been listening to the same songs over and over again for years now so that I can be more productive whenever I feel like getting stuff done.

You'll want to find songs that make your brain focus on the task at hand and block out anything else that may distract you from doing your thing. You can create your own deep focus playlist by playing music that inspires you and makes your blood pump faster every time it starts playing in your ears.

Improving your focus during meetings

Meetings - virtual or in person - can be a great way to share important information with others. They are great for brainstorming, for reaching consensus and for planning what you're going to do next.

But most of us don't always do a great job of focusing in meetings because we're distracted by our thoughts about what we want to say or how the meeting is going. Instead, we need to learn how to focus in meetings and not let our minds wander off from the conversation that we've been invited to be a part of.

- Practice active listening

The difference between active listening and passive listening is that you are awake and alert when you're in active listening mode. You should never just assume that you know what the speaker is saying even if it's someone who has been in your team for a few years now. To practice active listening, do the following:

- Never interrupt the speaker

- Make sure to not be distracted by other things – your surroundings, your office mates or anything else that may be distracting you from actively listening to the speaker.
- Take notes on what you're learning from the speaker so that after the meeting is over, you can review what they've shared with everyone else.
- Ask questions that will help you remember the things that were shared with everyone else.

Summaries are not an effective way to remember what has been said during a meeting because it makes you focus on the physical material instead of what's important and vital for each individual in the meeting. You're much better off just listening to everything that was shared with everyone else and taking notes of those things so that when you review your notes later, you have a clearer picture of what was discussed in the meeting.

- Ask questions

2. Seek clarification when you're confused

If you're baffled by something that was just shared with everyone else in the meeting, then don't be afraid to ask questions. What you need to do is provide additional information when something is unclear to you so that you can learn more about it and remember everything that has been said. Sometimes, we don't know what we don't know. It's OK not to understand something at first glance because it's easy for the brain to process new information once it has been broken down into small parts. Keep on asking lots of questions until everything makes sense. Contribute to the discussion by sharing what you've learned with everyone else.

3. Remember to stay focused on the task at hand

I find that I have a hard time staying focused in meetings simply because I'm trying to think of what I want to say next and how the meeting should be handled. If you're doing this, then it's important for you to understand that your job is not just to talk but also listen and learn from other people.

When you're in a meeting, it's usually because you want to be there and contribute something valuable so being able to focus is of utmost importance for everyone attending that meeting. Remember to keep yourself focused on the topic at hand and visualize what's going to be discussed so that you don't end up wasting your time on things that you're not interested in.

Are emails distracting you?

To most of us, emails are a good way to keep in touch with important people. We rely on emails, and we often check our inboxes on a regular basis just to find out if there's something important that needs our attention.

Can you imagine your day without checking your email inbox? The reason why we always check our email is because it's the only way for us to know what's going on when we're not around. It keeps us connected to other people, it helps us build relationships, it shows us how much work we need to get done and it gives us the motivation that we need in order to become successful in life.

It's the preferred commu8nication channel in most workplaces. The problem is that we let our email inbox overwhelm us instead of using it as a tool to help us get more work done. When this happens, we find ourselves pulling out our phones and checking our email message inbox every 30 minutes just to see what's new. How can we avoid this?

- Schedule your day so you know what to do next

This will only work if you're organized and if you have a clear list of things that need your attention. Usually, the best way for you to improve your focus is by learning how to become organized. Don't use your email as a to-do list. Instead, use your to-do list as a way for you to schedule your day so you know what to prioritize. Avoid interruptions and focus on what's important for the rest of your day by scheduling everything else after you're done with your most important task.

When you check your email every 30 minutes, you're more likely to respond immediately instead of letting the message sit in your inbox until you've accomplished all of the tasks that are on your to-do list.

Remember that most of us have a hard time resisting an urge. The human brain loves novelty and when we see something new, we want it right away. This is the shiny object syndrome where we get excited whenever we see a new email message in our inbox. This makes it hard for us to ignore and resist the urge to check our email inbox so it's important for you to schedule your time and days so you know when you can check your email.

- Schedule time to check your email

When you're checking your email, do it on a specific day at a specific time. This way, an attractive and important looking message will still catch your attention by the time that day arrives because that's what you're looking forward to. Avoid checking your email as soon as you come back to your desk. This will make it hard for you to focus on the task at hand because you're likely to be interrupted by something that's more important than the task at hand. Now, don't get me wrong, this is only if there are more important tasks that need your attention. If not, then go ahead and check your email and schedule everything else after it's done.

Unprofessional, annoying, and distracting co-workers

In every office there's that one person who always stands out from the crowd. He or she is that annoying person who you really want to punch in the face but have to endure because there's no other way for you to get your work done without dealing with him or her.

Some unprofessional and annoying co-workers will go out of their way to make others feel uncomfortable so that they can prove their worth by getting a promotion or a higher salary. However, these people shouldn't be tolerated for long because your productivity will drop, and this makes it hard for you to earn more money and progress in your career. It becomes harder for you to get things done if you're forced to deal with an unprofessional obnoxious co-worker. How can we politely deal with annoying co-workers?

- Talk to your supervisor

Some people are just plain inconsiderate. They don't care about the work they're doing, and they clearly don't mind whether their co-workers feel uncomfortable with the way they behave. It's important for you to get a second opinion before you decide to confront this person because you don't want to end up doing something that you're going to regret in the future. Your supervisor is there for a reason, so try talking to him or her first and see what he or she thinks should be done. If that didn't work, then it's time for you to talk it out with this person. Don't do anything that will embarrass anyone unless it's really necessary. When dealing with an annoying co-worker, don't talk behind his or her back and never lie about the situation. If your co-worker is doing something wrong, say it directly to him or her.

If your co-worker doesn't like what you have to say, then it's best if you just let it go. Don't spend time gossiping about him or her with other people because this will only make things worse. Try to think of a more creative way for you to deal with this person in a more productive and discreet way.

- Ignore him or her

This works best if the person you need to deal with is someone you only see in your office. When you ignore them and they can't take it anymore, they'll eventually get tired of waiting for you to acknowledge them and will leave on their own. Once they're gone, focus on other things that need to be done for your company because you're more productive when people aren't distracting you from what's important. Don't give into the urge of confronting this person because it can make your co-workers view you as a troublemaker who always causes problems.

Don't pay attention to annoying coworkers and they may take the hint that you're busy, so they'll stop bothering you. Don't give into the urge to confront unprofessional and vulgar co-workers because it doesn't solve the problem. Instead, try ignoring them and see if they get the hint or if they're going to insist on talking to you no matter what happens. You can also work from home for a day or two so you can get some things done without dealing with these people.

CHAPTER 12: RECHARGING

Our willpower is finite. The more you use it, the more tired you get. When you don your cape and the hustle and bustle of the day begins, it's hard to remember how important it is to recharge yourself. As Batman, who spent most of his nights fighting crime, always tells Robin to rest so that he can be ready for the next night. The same thing applies to us. If you don't recharge and get rest regularly, it'll be hard for you to get the most out of your workday.

What's burnout?

Burnout happens when we're constantly overworked and it's a serious issue that can be avoided with the proper planning. Burnout is your body telling you to slow down and rest because it's tired from all of the effort that you're putting into your work. It makes it hard for you to do anything at full capacity. When you're burnt out, your willpower is almost depleted and it's hard to make decisions. Your drive to do anything becomes almost nonexistent. Now does this sound like something you want to have?

Burnout can be caused by many things, but I'll name only three, overworking yourself, poor diet, and no exercise. Overworking yourself is the main reason people burn out. It's the thing that makes your willpower deplete even the most motivated of us. You might be inspired and on fire with a lot of energy, but you push yourself too hard so that your motivation burns out right with you as well. You might think you can get away with pushing your body to places that it isn't meant to go. It might work for a while but eventually, you'll have to slow down or risk burning out permanently.

When I talk about poor diet, I'm talking about the unhealthy foods that you eat. You know what I'm talking about, the super sugary snacks, the fatty fast-food burgers, and soda. Those things are terrible for your health and will make you feel like crap if consumed too much of in a single sitting. A diet rich in fiber, vitamins and healthy fats will help sustain your energy throughout the day and help you do a better job at work.

Another thing that causes burnout is exercise. You might think that you're too tired to go to the gym or for a run but if you skip it then your stamina will be affected negatively. When you exercise, your body uses more oxygen to function and even if it doesn't feel like it, exercise is an excellent way to recharge yourself. We lead sedentary lives and it's a good idea to try and stay active every day.

If you're burned out, then it's important to stop and make a change. You need to consider whether you'll be able to handle the workload that you're under. If not, then you should let your supervisor know that you're having trouble keeping up with the pace of the job. Don't be afraid to take a break for a few days or weeks if needed. Don't beat yourself up if something doesn't come together right away because there's always room for improvement. Work smart and work hard but remember that nothing is more important than your health in this world.

It can happen anytime, but burnout is most dangerous when creativity comes into play. When you're burned out, your creativity might be at a low point. What you need to do is make sure that you get some time alone, take a mental health day, or find a different job. Don't just let yourself burn out because it can have adverse effects on your personal relationships and health if left untreated.

Scheduling 'worry time'

'Worry time' is scheduled specifically for you to worry about anything that you're having trouble with. It means that you're going to take some alone time to think about what's troubling you and come up with a solution that can be used at a future date. The most important thing is that it gives you time to think. With this, we'll give ourselves the freedom of thinking and considering new ways to get around issues that have troubled us in the past.

Scheduling 'worry time' is a cognitive-behavioral therapy technique where you're encouraged to schedule time specifically for you to think about your problems so that you can come up with solutions to your troubles. This type of therapy is used by people with anxiety and depression because it gives them the space they need to clear their mind and come up with all of the possible solution. Instead of worrying while working, while studying, or while doing other things, the person schedules the time to think.

The benefits of this type of therapy are many, including:

- It becomes easier for you to deal with everyday worries and problems.

- You can solve your problems when you have time, regardless of whether you're having trouble in regards to work or personal problems.

- It keeps your brain from focusing on anything but dealing with its own thoughts, which improves concentration and leads to better memory.

- You'll stay calmer and less stressed out so that you won't be distracted during work and other activities.

Exercise for the body is music for the soul

Exercise provides us with more than just physical health benefits, it also has a positive effect on our mental health. Exercise is scientifically proven to affect the mind positively and it doesn't just benefit your body. It also helps boost your mood, keeps you more attentive, and even makes you smarter. We're most interested in how it affects our productivity. What do you feel after exercise? Do you feel more awake? More focused? More determined?

The reason for this is that it releases a hormone called dopamine. Dopamine makes us feel good and when we exercise, it's released into our bloodstream. We're rewarded with a sense of euphoria and anything at hand will seem easier to get done.

Aside from that, when you exercise, your brain releases endorphins. Endorphins are responsible for making you feel less pain and can also help you deal with emotional problems. You get to relax, and your body feels rejuvenated afterwards so that you'll have the extra energy to complete tasks easily.

Exercising is one of the most enjoyable things that we can do because it doesn't just make us feel those positive effects and it also helps our bodies stay healthy for many years to come.

A brisk walk during lunch, a trip to the gym during your break and sports activities with your friends. These are just some of the ways that you can unwind yourself. Just be sure that when you do exercise, it doesn't just involve sweating it out at the gym. Exercising can come in many forms and there are tons of ways to get some activity in your life. As long as it's getting your heart rate high, you're improving your health and helping yourself to feel more energetic, the more open to other activities you become.

Recharging when you're emotionally drained

When you're emotionally drained, you might not be able to get the job done. It's easy to lose yourself and the ability to focus when things go wrong. Something might just happen that leads you to feel bad about yourself, or it could be a series of events that causes you emotional problems. Either way, we need to recharge ourselves when this happens because we simply can't let it take over our lives. We should take the time to step back and address any underlying problems.

If you're feeling emotionally burned out, it's important that you recognize that feeling and deal with it systematically because if not, then more problems will pop up in your life in due time.

Emotionally draining things may include; having a baby, a high-pressure job, intense schooling, or divorce among many others. Whatever the case may be, these are things that we should prioritize over anything else in our lives because it will end up affecting us physically, mentally, and emotionally.

You need to take the time to let yourself feel how you're feeling and learn how to deal with your problems. You'll be surprised at how many little things that caused you stress actually solved themselves if you just sit down and think about them.

- Focus on the present

When things go wrong or you feel bad about yourself, it's good to focus on the present. Don't let that moment last longer than it should and remember why you got into the situation in the first place. It's good to stop and think about what happened, how it made you feel, and why it was so traumatic for you. It is important that we recover from these moments without feeling like we're losing our minds. Don't allow your stress level to get out of control because if not, things will start getting worse rather than better.

Stay in the present moment. If you're feeling down, just stop and realize that you've been through things before and got through them. You'll be surprised at how many times you've faced the same ordeals in the past and have recovered from them. You should do this to let yourself relax because stress usually happens when we try to fix something that we can't fix.

Dealing with emotional problems is a lot better than letting it take over your life because it doesn't matter as much as we think it does. We shouldn't waste our time worrying about things that won't make any difference in our lives in the long run.

You could talk to a therapist or to a friend. Share your feelings and problems so that they can help you. Counselors take the time to think about what's going on in your life and how you can make it a bit easier for yourself. They talk about how to make things better, or at least not as bad as they were before.

- Be realistic

You need to realize that there's nothing you can do about a situation that caused (or is currently causing) you stress because it's probably out of your control. You should work with what you have rather than trying to do something about something when we all know that it will never happen.

Be real to yourself. What's draining you? What are you doing to cope with the stress? Are you partying? Are you taking drugs or drinking a lot of alcohol? You may be doing one or all of these things, but we all know that nobody is able to stop these things from happening.

When things get too much for you and it's becoming hard for you to function, don't let yourself become overwhelmed. Endure things so that you don't break yourself down. Sometimes, the best thing for us to do is endure until everything gets resolved.

- Positive self-talk

You need to find positive things about yourself because that's what helps you feel better. It's good to talk to yourself in a positive way when you're feeling bad about yourself. When this happens, you will feel better about yourself and quit feeling so depressed about what others think of you.

Positive things should be said like; "I've done this before, and I can do it again." Or "There are times that I can't control and there are times that I can." Use mantras which will activate some type of emotional response in your body. For example, "I can do this" or "I'm going to make it till the end." Positive self-talk is an effective way of calming down even if you're feeling down. Talking to yourself in a positive manner always helps with how you feel about yourself.

When things are bad and we feel down, it's good that we talk to ourselves in a manner that influences those feelings that we have inside of us to change. We need to be able to say things like; " I'm strong enough to get through this and I can do this." when we feel down.

Affirmations make us feel better about ourselves when we're feeling down. If you say it out loud, it will help you feel better about yourself faster because your brain will accept the thoughts that we are saying to ourselves as real. You need to repeat something like; " I am a survivor of my past and I can do this." or "I am intelligent" before working on a project so that your brain will accept the thoughts into your subconscious mind faster than usual.

CHAPTER 13: STAYING ON TRACK

They say that staying in shape is harder than getting in shape. Maybe that's true. Consistency and commitment seem to be the key for staying on top of things. The challenge for most people is keeping with the program despite the fact that life has a way of getting in the way. Getting started is one thing. Staying focused on your goal is another.

It's all about sticking with it and staying on track, no matter what. People who succeed are those who stay on track and don't let other things get in their way. Remember that you need to do some research and work out a plan for yourself. Once you have the plan all figured out, stick with it no matter what happens.

The most important thing is to have a goal set for yourself so that you can succeed at staying on track. People who manage to stay focused will ultimately be successful at whatever they try to do and accomplish whatever they put their mind to.

Let's say that you've implemented a winning productivity regimen where you meet your goals every day with a few hours to spare. How do you stick with the plan? Let's look at how you can do it.

Have an accountability system

The 'man in the mirror' method we discussed in chapter 4 where you write down what you've achieved at the end of everyday is a great way to keep on track. It helps you stay focused and on schedule by knowing that you need to get your goals done by the end of the day. You should tell a friend or family member about what you've accomplished in order to help yourself stay on track. That way, you'll be accountable for what you're supposed to do.

It will feel a lot better if someone else knows about your plan to accomplish something. They'll keep reminding you of your goal and it will make it seem more real than before because all of a sudden there will be someone else who is depending on you also.

What accountability do you have for yourself? If you have an accountability partner, what can they do to help you?

Write down every task that you need to accomplish. If there are things that you haven't done, write them down too. Then, make a list of each one of the tasks and their priority. Make sure to work on the most important ones first before working on the others. You may have a lot of tasks to do but don't stress about it. At the end of the day, you will revisit this list. Check off the tasks that are already done and write down everything that you've done. Include what you're going to do tomorrow, next week and the next few weeks.

This is a great way of staying on track because it tells you what you need to do so that one day after you finish a task, you'll be able to move on to the next task. Remember that most people only work on one thing at a time so don't feel guilty if this is your approach.

Goal tracker apps are also great for reminding you of your goals and helping you stay on track. If you're staying on track, you will have more time to enjoy life than before.

Rewarding yourself is a great way of having motivation for doing something. You should reward yourself for all the little things that you do to stay on track. For example, if you get your plan together and finished everything that you needed to do that day, reward yourself by doing something nice like taking an afternoon read or going out with friends to a restaurant or something like that. Doing this will make it easier for you to start when the next day comes around.

Celebrate the small wins. Did you wake up without hitting the snooze button? Make a cup of coffee to celebrate that. Did you complete at least one task before bed? Have some chips and watch a movie instead. These are the little wins that make you feel better about yourself and how you're doing.

Celebrate your achievements by taking pictures of yourself or sharing them with others on social media sites. These will be great reminders for when you look back on your plan in the future. Doing this will also make it easier for you to remember more about what's going on with your plan because it will be fresh in your mind at all times, even though it's been a while since the last time you did it.

Rewards are great ways of giving yourself motivation. What can you do to celebrate your achievements?

When people fail to accomplish their goals, it's usually because they gave up too soon. You probably know people who are good at accomplishing things but give up when things don't go their way. If you stay committed to what you're trying to do, then you won't have to worry about giving up.

Handling failure and setbacks

Your productivity journey won't be an easy one. The truth is that life gets in the way of things, and we don't always have everything planned out perfectly. Sometimes it happens when we least expect it and we're not capable of handling what's going on. There are many things that could go wrong so we need to be prepared for all of them.

For example, if you've been working on a project for a while but got sidetracked, then you might need to write a new plan or change your initial plan entirely because you'll need to make up for the time that you lost when you got sidetracked.

Life will give you random kicks in the pants and that's okay. Death is real and it's going to happen one day so you might as well make the most of your time while you're still alive. You need to take each day as it comes and prepare yourself for all the stuff that could happen.

Get upset at yourself if something bad happens to you. It's important to get upset with yourself if something happens to mess you up because then you will know that there is room for improvement. It's good to be prepared for everything in life because life gives you random things that knock us off track sometimes. That's okay because life isn't meant to be perfect, and we're allowed some mistakes here and there.

Everyone errs. Winners have a strategy to deal with it. They get back on their feet and make up for the time that they lost. Don't worry about what you did wrong. Just make up for it and continue on your way.

Getting upset about things because you failed doesn't do anyone any good. You have to admit that you failed and try not to let this happen again. This will help to improve your productivity because now you have something to work towards in the future when things get tough again.

Sometimes, people fail because they don't do enough research before deciding on a plan of action.

How do we handle failures and setbacks?

- Anticipate setbacks

Before starting on any plans, you should always anticipate things that could go wrong. If you do this beforehand, then it will be easier for you to get back on track when something does happen. For example, if you decide to take a vacation and plan out your meals in advance, what will you do when the kitchen that you're renting from is broken? You'll need to change your plan entirely or come up with something else because the kitchen isn't working so now cooking meals is going to be tough.

You'll need to adapt. To be successful in life, you must always anticipate the worst-case scenarios.

- Change your perspective

If you fail on one thing, then that's okay. Failure is part of life and it's meant to teach us things so that we can do better the next time that we try again. If you fail, then write down what went wrong so that you can take a look at it and learn from your mistakes. There's a lesson to be learned from every experience so don't be frustrated when you fail on something.

- Try again

When something happens, you have to change your plan and try again. If something goes wrong, then that's fine because you're learning something along the way. Do what needs to be done to get back on track and try once more. Remember, failure is not a bad thing and it's not going to happen often if you take the proper steps into account. It's all part of life and we should accept this rather than getting upset about it.

- Assess the situation

Whenever something happens, you need to assess the situation. Don't just sit around and do nothing because that's wasting time. See what needs to be done and do it as fast as you can. If you make a mistake, then learn from it. Use this as an opportunity to improve in the future and make up for all that time that you lost when it happened.

Setbacks are okay if they don't happen too often. Once something goes wrong, then try again and don't worry about what went wrong before because it's not worth the time of worrying about those things when there's so much else to do in life.

- Surround yourself with positive people

Positivity is contagious. So is negativity. Do you want to surround yourself with negative people who will bring you down and make you feel bad about yourself? Or do you want to surround yourself with positive people who are going to help you out so that you can accomplish more in life?

It's important that we surround ourselves with the right kind of people no matter what we're doing in life. You need to focus on the things that are going right because then it will be easier for us to keep our eyes on the ball and not get sidetracked by all the stuff that comes our way unexpectedly.

We learn from our mistakes. There's no such thing as a failure, only feedback with a purpose. You need to learn from things that happen to you and use them to your advantage so you can do better the next time around.

- Don't get frustrated with yourself

When something bad happens, don't get frustrated with yourself because it doesn't help anyone. It will actually cause problems in your life and there's nothing good that comes out of getting upset over things that don't even matter in the end. When someone else fails on something, be positive towards them and don't hold it against them because it only makes it harder for everyone involved including yourself.

Don't take things personally. People often take things that happen in life personally because they don't understand that it was just a random thing that happened and there's nothing we can do about it. You need to be in control of yourself so when something bad happens, you won't let it affect you because there's nothing good that comes out of letting little problems get to you. Life is not perfect, but the one who tries to achieve perfection is. Don't try too hard because then you'll only end up failing, which is no fun.

Getting back on track

There are ways that you can use to get back on track. Here are some of those ways:

- Check in with yourself

When something upsets you, check in with yourself and see if there's any part of you that is overreacting. Are you really upset or are you just upset that things didn't go according to plan? If you're upset because things didn't go as planned, then maybe this is a sign that you need to change your plan.

Look back on your life and think about what things have been the most successful for you so that you can continue doing more of those things in the future. For example, maybe the career path that you chose was not a good one. Looking back on it now, can you see any way that it could've been better? Maybe if you had looked for more information about it beforehand? It's okay to make mistakes as long as we learn from them and use them to our advantage so that we don't make those same mistakes again.

At the end of the day, we need to remember that not everything is going to go our way. We can have everything all planned out, but things are still going to happen that are unexpected. The only thing that we can do is to work hard and try again; after all, we learn so much more from our failures as opposed to our successes.

Had a rough day? Take a power nap and recharge yourself because that's what it's all about. When you feel like you need a break, then get some sleep. There's nothing good that comes out of being tired and trying to do things that are difficult on your own. Take a power nap and when you wake up, then go out there and try again. Before you respond to people's emotions, take a moment to look at where those emotions are coming from. Sometimes it's just a product of the way we were raised or sometimes it's because of past experiences or maybe even a premonition.

Sometimes, we feel that there's no need to let go of something that is causing us pain because it will never happen again. The truth is, most of the time, things turn out differently than we expect them to be. Sometimes, those previous situations are not a big deal in our lives right now and sometimes they have turned into something that is much better than expected. When you don't let go of what you're holding on to, it's like we live our entire lives in fear of something that hasn't even happened yet.

Embrace imperfection. We all have imperfections. We're not perfect and we're not meant to be. If we hold on to these things too tightly, it will only cause pain for ourselves. A little flexibility is good for us to allow us to be more open with our decisions. We need to give our dreams a chance, even if we fail at them in the beginning. The more we allow ourselves to try and fail, the closer we are getting to our dreams.

Be happy. Don't take things too seriously because you will hurt yourself in the end by trying harder than you need too and focusing on things that aren't even important to you or your life.

Putting it all together

At the start of this book, we took a crucial lesson from Isaac Newton. We saw that an object in motion stays in motion unless acted upon by an external force. Physics calls this momentum. When you're on a streak - be it a productivity streak where you get stuff done without procrastinating or a positive emotion streak where you're managing to stay positive no matter what - it's time to take a step back and notice what you're doing differently. Then you repeat it as often as you need to until it becomes automatic, and you don't even have to think about doing it anymore. You need to find a way to keep going, even when things go wrong or when you're in the depths of despair. This is where Newton's concept of momentum and his win-win principle come in.

Then, we took note of the lies that could be stopping us from reaching our goals. You might have been convinced by them.

This book is a manual for achieving optimum productivity. You've seen how habits can help you to perform at your best and how they can increase your productivity, but have you considered how they can also help increase your happiness? Almost everyone is using some form of an automated system to ensure that they are getting a full and uninterrupted workday. The fact that we have moved towards a work from home culture where we are spending more time close to our family, friends, loved ones but we're 'always working' is a challenge on its own. Traditionally, home was a place to relax and enjoy life. Your family, the dog, errands, laundry, and the TV may not understand that you're indeed busy. They've always known that when you come home after a long workday, you'd have time to relax, entertain them and spend time with them. Many of us struggle with balancing the demands of work with those of home life.

We saw how procrastination can have a serious detrimental effect on our lives. We saw how we can prevent this by using a to-do list and setting deadlines for ourselves. Many of us are so ignorant of what it takes to balance work with personal life and vice versa, because we go about it in a way that is all wrong.

We looked at how we can all make better decisions, how to learn from our mistakes, and how to manage the time that we have more effectively. We talked about breaking bad habits and the effortlessness of retaining the good ones. Managing stress was also discussed in the book as well as finding time and motivation to exercise. T regular breaks is vital for keeping your mind clear and your body healthy. We looked at the importance of not being a slave to technology.

Now that you know the importance of having balance in your life, you can use those habits to help you manage and work towards that balance. Finding the time to do so is going to require some sacrifices. You'll have to give something up and sacrifice it for what's truly important in life. Whether that is your job, your family, or something else entirely, it is important that you're honest with yourself about what needs to go and what needs to stay.

We discussed how we can all make better decisions, how to learn from our mistakes, and how to manage the time that we have more effectively.

What's next?

Go put into practice what you've learned. You can't learn anything from reading a book if you don't actually take any of it to heart. There will always be a challenge that comes up in life. Life is never exactly what we want it to be. When something goes wrong, we can either let it get the best of us or we can pick ourselves up, dust ourselves off and learn from our mistakes.

Being the most productive version of yourself is not something that happens overnight. It is something that you need to work at day in, day out, until one day you wake up and realise that you've become the person you were always meant to be. The only way you can make it happen is through practice. Start by making a conscious effort to become more productive.

It is important to note that not every single variation of productivity will have the same results for everyone. If you're applying the principles of this book to something different than what I have written, then go with it and make the most out of it!

At the end of it all, you'll look back on your life and you'll thank yourself for putting in the effort. You'll love the results!

Do you know someone who'd benefit from this book? If so, please feel free to share this book with them. The more people who are aware of what they could be doing to better themselves and their life, the better.

Thanks so much for reading!

Appendix

Over the years, I came to realize that productivity is a skill, just like tennis or playing an instrument. And like any skill, it requires practice to improve. After teaching my own and others' change efforts for about 6 years and watching people of all stripes struggle to become more productive, I realized that those who ended up becoming successful in the long run, followed a similar pattern.

The pattern I observed seems to be pretty universal, regardless of if it was a lawyer, businessperson or a programmer. So, I tried to put my observations into words, and I came up with four stages. These ideas are my way of phrasing what I saw, which may not be the same as what other people see. But here is my list:

I made a further realization that the real path to success lies in understanding these concepts. Once you understand them, you can get started on your journey. After all, it's easy to keep procrastinating when you don't know why you're doing something in the first place. Learning about these ideas will allow you to grasp the bigger picture behind productivity and goal setting. They will also help keep you from being discouraged and losing motivation on your way up that mountain of change.

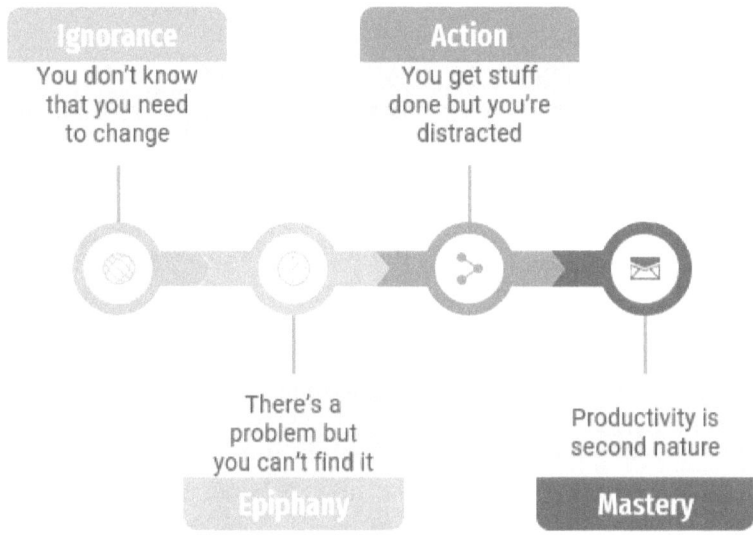

Phase 1: Ignorance

Everyone starts off at this phase where you're unproductive and you don't even know it. You don't even know you need to change in the first place. Your main problem is that your environment doesn't allow you to get started. You have to set goals, but work is unpredictable and there are many distractions.

You may not be aware of the benefits of productivity, so you don't know what's missing. So, at this stage, it's important to start by focusing on what you do know: the benefits of productivity and how they will help boost your productivity in the future.

Phase 2: Epiphany

You start to note that there are times when you're unable to 'get stuff done'. At this stage, it's important to start by identifying your main problems. If you're stuck, you will want to identify the root cause of your problem. Or, if you're procrastinating and unable to get started because change is stressful and uncomfortable...the root cause may be a lack of confidence in your ability to accomplish what needs to be done. There could also be pending tasks holding you back, or projects that you need to kickstart.

It may be that you simply need a little more motivation. Or even some basic structure, such as a daily to-do list. Either way, this stage is all about problem solving. It's about visualizing your goals and figuring out how to get there.

Phase 3: Action

At this stage, you're able to get stuff done but you're easily distracted. You can focus on the task at hand, but you have to keep reminding yourself to stay focused. You may even have to create strategies for staying focused and avoiding the distractions that come up during the day.

Phase 4: Mastery

You become like Neo in The Matrix, where you are literally "unplugged" from all distractions and you're able to focus on the task at hand without effort. This is where productivity and goal setting become second nature to you. You can go from task to task without any effort expended in staying on track. It's just like breathing; it's something that you do naturally, effortlessly and without thinking about it.

You're able to meet your goals without even thinking about it. It almost feels like you're in auto pilot mode where you just keep accomplishing task after task.

Attribution

Icons from Flat Icon

Business vector created by freepik - www.freepik.com

Infographic from slidesgo.com

www.ingramcontent.com/pod-product-compliance
Lightning Source LLC
Chambersburg PA
CBHW020907080526
44589CB00011B/474